Mo(u)rning Joy

a memoir

Kalan Chapman Lloyd

This book is for

Caswell,

and Jamie Sue,

and Jensen,

and Luke and Hope,

and Lily,

and Kingsley,

and Hayes,

and their brave, brave mamas and daddies

Mo(u)rning Joy: a memoir

2015 Lloyd Words trade edition

Published in the United States by Lloyd Words, LLC.

ISBN 978-1-312-93528-0
eBook ISBN 978-1-312-93528-0

Cover image: Christy Obalek
Typography: Carrie Ryan

Printed in the United States of America

Lloyd Words trade edition: October 2015

Visit the author at www.kalanchapmanlloyd.com
All scripture quotations, unless otherwise indicated, are taken from the Holy Bible, NIV.

Mo(u)rning Joy

a memoir

Kalan Chapman Lloyd

It's a weird green. Bright, sickly, electric. If you see it, you know. It's unmistakable. And indicative of only one thing. Those that don't know, have never seen it; might call it beautiful. If you know, you would never use that word.

If you run, you eventually have to come back. If you hunker down, you eventually have to climb out. It's almost impossible to stand out in it and face it.

It levels, razes, obliterates. It knows no class, income, race. It is quick, razor-sharp, and debilitating. The great equalizer in crippling devastation.

While you're running, while you're hunkering, in the middle of it all, you have no outside connection to the rest of the world.

In the aftermath, while you're climbing out, coming back, the tragedy creates bonds that wouldn't have otherwise existed. Crossing race, income, class.

After, in the morning, it will likely be a bright dusky blue, clear, crisp, feathered with white wisps. The birds will sing cheerfully; out of place, ironic, grating. But... If you can give up, give over, surrender, you will find the song is sweeter, clearer, crisper, more glorious, joyful. Borne out of a new knowledge, a new gratefulness, a new appreciation. For life.

Morning always comes. The things that emerge from the wreckage and remain are the ones that matter the most. They are of great importance, even if they make no sense at the time.

How do you find comfort in the chaos? You don't. How do you get the strength to rebuild? You don't. How do you see the joy in the morning? You don't.

You can't. *You* won't. It's impossible. *He* can. *He* will. The impossible.

"... weeping may last for the night,

but joy comes in the morning."

- Psalm 30:5

A Mom's Note:

Otherwise Known As

Ignorable Advice

Hey Mr. Grumpy Gills, when life gets you down, you know what you got to do? Just keep swimming.

– Dori, Finding Nemo

This is not a self-help book. I'm not qualified to give advice, offer tips, or tell you a five-step program for grieving. This is our story.

Yours. Theirs. His. Hers. Is different.

But. I've been asked. And I remember asking. So I have one piece.

Kalan Chapman Lloyd

Just keep going. Get up every day and acknowledge the pain and the place and vow not to be there a year later. Your pace is your own. One good friend told me, "I don't want this to define our family: this tragedy."

I wish I'd had those words. That's how I felt but couldn't quite see the clarity of that statement. You don't have to know how to get out of the cloud and fog you might be in. Just knowing you're in one and that you want to get out is enough. Just keep swimming. Even if it means you're just treading water. Just keep swimming.

The Best Laid Birth Plans

"When you reach the end of your rope, tie a knot and hang on."

– Typically attributed to Thomas Jefferson

This is stupid.

That's all I could think as I lay in the hospital bed waiting for the pill they'd shoved up under my cervix to dissolve and start the dilating to begin. This is stinkin' 2012 and they haven't figured out a way to get my dead baby out of my body without making me come to the labor and delivery ward of the hospital that I hadn't yet toured so I could deliver a stillborn infant just unlike the mamas next door. The mamas who were delivering healthy, live babies. Unlike my baby, who had been dead inside my body for at least two weeks.

I cursed that I'd gone to law school instead of medical school due to my little issue of fainting upon the sight of blood. Surely, if *I* had attended medical school and found out this was how they did this, *I* would have discovered some way to ensure that if a mother discovered her son was to be stillborn after a routine ultrasound, she could be knocked out and wake up skinnier than before.

Apparently, no one had thought of this super fabulous idea. No one, because I was currently laying in a hospital bed, my tearful husband annoying the crap out of me because he was having feelings, and I was trying to forget what feeling felt like. *This*, I had not factored into my birth plan.

It Gets Weird

"May you never feel what I then felt. May your eyes never shed such stormy, scalding, heart-wrung tears as poured from mine. May you never appeal to Heaven in prayers so hopeless and so agised as in that our left my lips."

– Charlotte Bronte *Jane Eyre*

The day before, we had gone to the medical center adjacent to the hospital for our twenty-four week OB appointment. We had an ultrasound scheduled at 9:45 that morning. They were very particular about us going to the ultrasound office before we set foot into the OB office. So particular that the nurses and office staff reminded us every time we had an ultrasound scheduled, and oozed irritation the day I'd forgotten and went to check in at their office first.

This was actually only our third ultrasound. Our first was our first appointment at eight weeks, a vaginal ultrasound (um, yuck, why had no one told me about this part?!) to ensure the little nugget was viable and on track growth-wise. The strong little heartbeat and perfectly shaped shrimp said he most definitely was. The second was to find out the sex of the nugget at twenty weeks.

He was a boy. I was shocked. My husband high-fived me in the elevator. We weren't set to have another ultrasound. That was it.

Apparently not, because when we finally saw our doctor she told us something was a little weird. Weird. She said it ever so nonchalantly, like when you forget to put a fork at one place when you set the table. Or when you get your sundae in the to-go lane, and go home to find there's no cherry. Or when your doctor tells you your kid is in the third percentile. Third mother-trucking percentile.

This might not have rocked my world, if I was short, petite or small in any way. We are not little people. We're pretty dang huge, actually. My husband has been in the 99th percentile since he was born, finally landing at 6'5" and 230 lbs. I myself rest comfortably at 5'9" and a solid, healthy 150. We were expecting a great big athlete, maybe softball player or basketball stud. I had expressed somewhat proud fear that I was going to birth a toddler. And now this chick was telling me I had a small kid?! Oh no she di-int.

But she followed up "weird" with "it's nothing to worry about." So she scheduled another ultrasound for our next appointment, just to make sure everything was okay and to see if maybe he'd had a growth spurt. Four weeks later, *weird* took on a whole new meaning.

Little Tiny Spiders

"Normal is an illusion. What is normal for the spider
is chaos for the fly."

– Morticia Adams

It took them forever to get to us. We were scheduled at 9:45 on a Monday morning. I had called in to my office and told my assistant I wouldn't come in until after the appointment. I wanted to stay home and leisurely take time to fix my hair, put on the lipstick with special powers, and move the folded laundry I had neglected from our living room to the drawers where it belonged. Husband had decided to meet me at the doctor's office.

After a forty-five minute wait, I finally told him to go back to his office. He had stuff to do and this was just a measly twenty-four week check-up. He declined, and five minutes later, they finally called us back.

Kalan Chapman Lloyd

They called me by my hyphenated name, which never failed to aggravate my husband. I was not in any way hyphenated, but because my office had requested we phase out my maiden name so as not to confuse clients, the human resources person who had updated my insurance hyphenated my name on all the documents. My husband was in fear our child would be born without his surname, but with a hyphenated version of both. As a family law attorney, he knew better, but I think it was more the principle of the thing.

When they called us back, I wondered if they called me by my "Mrs." moniker because they knew I was an attorney with a hyphenated name and thought I wanted respect or because my first name was so hard to pronounce. When we got to the ultrasound room, my husband confirmed by commenting that they were intimidated by my first name because they had called all the mothers before me by their first names.

He was often doing this, saying out loud exactly what I had been thinking. It was another way that solidified he was most definitely my "lobster" (lobsters mate for life, you know). We were infinitely annoying at parties. We were "that couple."

Grant and I had met in Geneva, Switzerland. Don't get jealous or whipped into a frenzy; it's not near as exciting as it may sound. After a clever game of ships in the night that apparently had lasted most of our lives, we finally met in another country studying abroad. It then took us another two years to actually go on a date. It then took my husband another two long years to propose (he likes to take his time). So while the courtship may sound dreamy, it was actually couched in logic and romantic calculation. We are lawyers, after all. Had God not spoken loud and clear about Grant being my future husband, I might have laughed. Grant and I are opposites in so many ways. But he *is* my lobster.

When I rolled down my maternity leggings and hiked up my two-sizes-bigger-than-before dress, the tech slapped the goo on and pressed the wand to my belly. Her first and only comment was, "Awwww, he's curled into a ball today."

18

After the fact, I kept thinking about the big, hairy, dead spider I'd found in the room I was redecorating for our nephews. I had never before taken note that spiders curled into balls when they die. All I could think was that I had a big, dead spider inside my body where my live, healthy, shrimpy baby used to be.

We heard nothing except the click of the measurements she took. Afterward, we would both express that we weren't sure if we were supposed to be hearing anything, but thought that we were, but thought, surely she would say something if we were. When the big, black band flashed across the bottom of the screen with nothing but gray nothingness, we knew. When the tech said she had to go call the doctor, we knew. When we asked her if something was wrong and she told us she wasn't allowed to say, we knew. As silent tears streamed down my husband's face and I told him not to panic, that we didn't know what was going on, we knew. Our dream, our expectation, our hopes that we'd wrapped into a tiny little person too small to even be able to live up to all those plans, was gone.

April Showers Bring May Babies

"I had the hardest time once he was buried. I remember crying into my husband's chest, "I don't want to be this person. This Mom with a baby in a grave. How do I handle that? How do I visit my baby and leave him over and over? I still don't know the answer."

– Mandy, Hayes' mama

Dear pregnant or future pregnant friends,

Don't expect me to come to your baby showers. I'll send a gift, I will. I probably won't have lovingly have chosen it, like I used to do, but I'll send one. The good news is: I'll never expect you to host a baby shower for me. In fact, you don't even have to worry about having to attend or send a gift to any future baby showers for me. I don't plan on having any. In fact, my plan for the next "if" pregnancy is to have the ultrasound person write boy or girl on a piece of paper, seal it in an envelope, and I'll give it to my mom and best friend. They can decorate the nursery behind my back while I'm in the hospital, hopefully giving birth to a live baby. If you feel overwhelmingly compelled to buy me something, contact them. You'll avoid getting hit this way.

Love,

The mom whose baby died in utero

Oddly, I've never been a particularly jealous or envious person. As a fat kid, I'd just decided to get skinny when it bothered me. I wanted clothes? I'd work to buy them. Someone's boyfriend? Eh, not meant to be. But after Cas died, that green-eyed monster was the monkey on my back. I got pregnant on the first try when they gave us the go-ahead. We used every method the Catholics, the doctors, and the Internet message boards tout. So yay us, right? You'd think, I would be grateful.

Heck to the no. A friend posted on Facebook that she was pregnant. Eye roll. A baby shower invite. A huffy sigh. Hosting a baby shower for a friend whose first child was stillborn. A three-hour crying jag. People with three kids. An uncomfortable heart tug. Baby announcement. A donut binge. Y'all, I was pregnant myself. I could/was/had ALL THESE THINGS.

It wasn't that I wanted to be them. I wanted to be the person before the thing happened. I wanted to be vapid and whine and complain about how much I hated being pregnant. I wanted to revel in the fact that my body performed a miracle (with God and my husband of course). I couldn't do it. I was jealous that *I knew*. I mention this a lot. Because it is so very important to my story. I needed to know. I needed to now be the person whose pretendabit is busted. Breaking was the only way I was ever going to be whole.

A ridiculously good-looking friend and I used to talk about boys. Boys who made bad decisions. She would say, in all her sage wisdom, that until you get down to the very bottom of the hole and live in the dirt awhile, you never completely crawl out.

My relationship with God was like that. Until I was at the very, very bottom of myself, with nowhere to go, but my fleeting hope and fake faith, I didn't need Him. I didn't need to be rescued.

Once I was there though, He dragged me out, whether I was ready or not.

Things That Are Gross For $200, Please

"For where two or three are gathered together in my name, there I am in the midst of them."

– Matthew 18:20

Do you know what they do to start this utterly barbaric "process?" They wrap sticks of dried, fake seaweed in wet gauze and jam it in your vagina. As many that will fit. Not fit comfortably, just fit. They call these luminaries, or something like that. It sounds so nice. Like when those cartoon townspeople set off those paper lanterns each year on the kidnapped princess's birthday in that faux-Rapunzel movie, *Tangled.* Just a little Disney, you know.

It's not nice. It's gross and disgusting and hurts like a sonofagun. I'd gone twenty-four weeks with nary a cramp or spot of blood in sight, and now it felt like the worst period ever and looked like I was peeing out watered down tar. Unbeknownst to me, when you mix betadine with urine, it's black. My nephews, obsessed with color combo outcomes, would've had a field day.

Then they send you home. To wait while you hope your cervix softens enough to actually start the induction process the next morning. So we went home, to wait, and cry. Grant cried anyway; I numbed out.

I'm a hospital veteran. To date, I've had eleven major surgical procedures, including a breast cancer scare. I was supposed to never run again and walk with a limp. Four times they told me this. I ran a 5k the week after I found out I was pregnant. For fun.

You'd think with all this experience and flat-out toughness, I would feel comfortable in hospitals. I don't. I hate them. The mere stepping foot inside one, even to visit people, makes me weak-kneed and dizzy.

But I'm also a long-time, card-carrying member of the suck-it-up club, because throughout my childhood, that was the only way to get through the pain. So I went into that place. I pulled a Scarlett. Tomorrow was another day, and I'd think about it tomorrow. If I could just get through tomorrow, I could think about the next tomorrow. And if I could take each tomorrow one at a time, I would have to think about the endless string of tomorrows stretched out in front of me without my son, who I'd envisioned as tall and broad-shouldered like his daddy, with a perfect nose like his mother, legs built like his grandfather, handsomely aristocratic features like his grandmother, and blond and brown eyed, like his other grandmother and cousin. In my head, I'd never pictured a baby-baby, only this blond, athletic, hazel-eyed man.

We had decided to name him Caswell Thomas, a family name times two. Caswell was a long-lost ancestor, famous for building churches in England and somewhere in the South. Thomas was his daddy's middle name. We expected him to be a church builder, literally, figuratively, however. But we put that on him. That expectation that because of his name, that's what he would do.

Honor God in that way. I read *Pillars of the Earth* to prepare myself to be the mother of a church-builder, in the literal sense. Church-building is hard, y'all. What were we thinking? Secretly, selfishly, I hoped his contribution to the kingdom would be in a non-literal, safe way, down the street from his mama.

But alas, here I was, lying in a hospital bed, waiting. I wanted to focus on the physical pain, so I wouldn't have to think about our little future church-builder, Cas, not living up to his namesake here with me. Building churches, far, far away from his mama.

Chipped Toenail Polish

"I will not cause pain, without allowing something new to be born, says the Lord."

– Isaiah 66:9

We got up at 4:30 the next morning to be at the hospital by 6:00 a.m. We went to the wrong place first, and after being directed to labor and delivery, checked in. We didn't know what to say.

We're here for an induction for our dead baby. We're here to deliver, but our baby is dead.

I felt not good enough to be there. I felt like a failure as a mother because I hadn't managed to come to the hospital in full delivery mode, with my baby ready to meet this world kicking and screaming. Once they figured out who we were (the hyphen and my maiden name were mercifully gone at this point), she led us to labor and delivery room "1," marked by a taped photo of black roses above the door. A morbid, pitying, mocking *photo* of flowers.

I changed into the hospital gown. I used the bathroom, wiping away more watery, black tar, dabbing so as not to disturb the dang seaweed. I sat on the hospital bed. I took off my ugly ski socks, examining my toes and their chipped polish. My pedicure was several weeks old and damaged by the fact that I'd had my nephews with me at the time and wasn't paying attention. I had slipped on loafers too soon after. I was planning on both a mani and pedi two weeks before my due date, just in case, and then a week before if there was still time, so I could meet my baby with nice hands and feet. The best laid plans…

I hadn't cried since the day before.

Zen I Was Not

"It's okay to be sad."

– Brittany, Jamie Sue's mama

The doctor came in after I'd been intravenously tubed and blood pressure cuffed. My husband and father left. My mom held my hand. They put me in stirrups and, with difficulty, pulled out the black, wet gauze-wrapped faux seaweed. The doctor praised me; it had worked well. My cervix was softer. Hoo-freakin'-rah.

I let all the words, and touches and emotions float by. This is something they teach you in yoga, which my grandma had forced me to start thirteen years before, to defy the limping prediction. They teach you to let everything float by. However, I wasn't proactively letting everything go. I was purposely numbing myself to it all. This, I thought while they tried their best to be kind in their poking and prodding, was kind of the antithesis of yoga.

The doctor then, with two gloved fingers, showed me a tiny pill that was to be placed under, behind my cervix to help it dissolve. It was supposed to start dilation. It hurt. At least I still felt pain.

A few hours later, in labor, cramps going strong, contractions beginning, they offered me the drugs. I'm usually pretty opposed to pain medication. I have a high tolerance for pain and loathe feeling out of sorts, or any other side effects. We, and by "we," I mean "I," was planning to go drug-free for his birth. You know, yoga breathing and stick biting; that was my plan.

I didn't know how much pain I was in at that point. With my two subsequent babies, I can remember the full force and the up-front, in-your-face pain that comes from an induction (and probably a natural birth I'm sure, but I'll never know). I recall vividly both the moments when I cried "uncle," waved the white flag, and threw the proverbial towel at my husband's head with Cowboy and Sassy Girl. With Cas, it just seemed like the right thing to do at the time. Not because of the pain, but because they told me I could. I should.

So when they offered, my guts kind of hurt, my kid was dead and I thought, what the hey. Big mistake. Huge.

I get migraines when I relax. Other people get them when they're tense, or when they eat chocolate or have wine. I get them when my body lets go of anxiety too quickly. This is probably a sign of how whacked out I am; that I run more effectively on stress than relaxation. I promise this is not on purpose.

So when they pumped some super narcotics into my IV, I got an immediate high. Like rush to the head, instantly loopy, toes couldn't curl if they wanted to, pleasantly nice and numb, duh-runk. And then about five minutes later the high turned into a bad trip. I got seriously puke-y and grabbed the trashcan. I was hot and sweaty. Then the migraine set in. Holy balls. Of all the things that could be happening, that was the worst. Just kidding. The worst thing was that they ran out of diet Shasta and I had to drink real.

Their solution? More of that funky drug. Outcome? Same reaction, migraine intensified. They then decided that I must be

31

having a reaction to the narcotics (ya think?), so I couldn't have any more. They brought me Tylenol for my migraine. Gee thanks, for the bandaid to put on my bullet hole, I appreciate it.

We were eight hours in, I'd had two rounds of super trippy narcotics, two extra strength Tylenol, two rounds of that cute little pill shoved into my nether regions. My "progress" had been checked at least five times. I had the mother of all headaches and my dead little spider was no closer to GETTING THE HELL OUT OF MY BODY than yesterday when she'd rammed seaweed into my yoohoo. How utterly fabulous.

Then they sent in the nun.

I Didn't See A Wimple

"We're here for a reason. I believe a bit of the reason is to throw little torches out to lead people through the dark."

– Whoopi Goldberg

She was no Mother Theresa. She seemed like a nice lady, truly. She, along with every other person with a badge that day, told me that if I wanted to hold the baby, bathe the baby, sit with the baby, I could. It usually helped.

Crap on a stick, are you kidding me lady? I have enough sense to know my child is in Heaven; this is just his body, I thought, clinging to my righteous indignation and throwing a little of the blame her way. There wasn't any sense in logically spreading it around, people. I don't want to see his body. I don't want to touch it. I want it out of me so that I can go on with my life. She kept looking at me imploringly, like I should be crying or saying something. I wanted to smack her. I let her pray for me instead.

This is what they do, y'all. There is an itemized checklist they use, as gently as they can, to try to get you to appropriately grieve your loss and your child. I'm sure four out of five psychiatric professionals approve of this method. It is a macabre, disturbing urging they all begin to almost chant. It is a time to make memories. A short, short, terrible time to make the worst kind of memories.

I try not to hold onto regrets and bad decisions. Rearview mirror be darned! Bring me windshield or bring me milkshakes! But not saying goodbye to Caswell's physical body is one I toy with quite often. It would have made no difference I know, but maybe I would have alleviated some of my guilt and wonder if I'd held him. Personal decision and one I have to live with, but in that moment, I clung hard to the fact that he wasn't there. He was already in Heaven and mourning his physical body would do me nothing. I didn't want to see the brokenness of him on earth. I wanted to wait and see his glorious body one day. It didn't seem honorable to meet him that way when I knew another happier meeting awaited us.

The nurses were kind enough to ignore me and take pictures. They took a picture of his feet. His precious, skinny feet. I never knew what he looked like. My mom is the only one of us that did that. She felt it was important to pray over him, so her recollection is the only idea I have of what he looks like. Like his daddy, if it matters.

The picture of Caswell's feet is hanging in our hallway. Along with pictures of the other four of us. And a big sign singing the importance of a family. It's macabre. It's disturbing. To have that hanging next to the shiny, bright, faces of the two here with us. But it's important. *He's* important. He exists. He was the beginning of the story.

There are things you do as the parent of a child you never got to meet. Things that others would only describe as weird. Like keeping your son's ashes in your nightstand. Like trying to change his name at the eleventh hour. Like sleeping with a shawl some little old ladies prayed over while they knitted during your next pregnancy because you think it will keep your baby safe. Like wearing five fertility bracelets for the duration of your pregnancy, even after you've been knocked up for the second time in record time. Like keeping pregnancy tests in your purse so you can pee on sticks at weddings, in airports, and convenience store bathrooms. I mean, I don't know anyone who does any of these things, but dang, all that just sounds plain creepy.

Pony Up

"Courage is being scared to death and saddling up anyway."

– John Wayne

When I was ten, I broke my arm riding bareback on my horse. It's probably a testament to how spoiled I was that my daddy went out and got me my veryownhorsethankyouverymuch during my own version of almost every girl's "horse phase." Princess might very well have been a mule. She wasn't mean, per se, but was only interested in doing what Princess wanted to do. Imagine the result when a child who thought she was in control of most everything around her attempted to command such a horse.

I didn't work with her enough. She probably needed to have been worked every day. I was good if I went up against her once a week. I don't remember being not afraid of horses, but I must not have been that afraid before the fall, because I would go off by myself in the field, find her, bridle her and attempt to bring her back to the house. It didn't work out all that often. I think I lost two of the pink and purple lead ropes my dad had bought for me. We ended up just leaving the bridle and bit on her most of the time, which wasn't a choice I would have made.

So one Sunday afternoon when I was feeling empowered, I had my dad hook up the lead rope like reins. He hoisted me up onto her bare back, her freshly brushed hair tickling my bare legs, and I took off toward my grandparent's house, eager to show my Papa what I'd done.

That past month, Princess had been hanging out in one of Papa's upper pastures, close to the house. She was old, so we'd decided to pamper her some. And it was easier to catch her if we didn't have to find her.

Close to my grandparents, a breeze picked up, and she got a whiff of her food. Like most pampered princesses, she didn't want to work, only eat and laze around. So when she smelled the comforts of home, she took off. Right toward the barbed wire fence that housed such comforts.

No amount of me pulling on the reins, shouting "whoa," or taking deep breaths slowed her down.

After the incident, everyone would say, "Kalan fell off her horse." I jumped y'all. I saw that barbed wire and even a chubby kid knows that's a model career killer. I bailed right off that fat, sassy thing and landed on my left humerus, causing the bone to break and then shift so the two pieces lay against each other, muscle tissue scattering.

Shock sets in after a bone break, so the pain wasn't really an issue in that moment. I was most concerned about that mean ole mule coming back to step on me. So I started scooting toward the corral to protect myself so she wouldn't get me. And hollering and screaming for my daddy. It's always been interesting to me that in that moment, I wanted my daddy. My mama had always been the comforting one. But when you fall, um, jump, off your very tall horse and are fearful for another broken bone, you holler for daddy.

He came running, yelling for my mom to get the truck. She didn't see any blood, and wasn't impressed with my unapparent injury, so it took her a minute to mind my daddy. Maybe I was misreading the comforting parent after all. Hmmm.

They loaded me up on my daddy's lap, with him holding the broken arm in place against me so nothing else would move around, and headed down the dirt road to the city hospital. Not a hopping place on a Sunday, mind you, but they took just too long enough to make my daddy ticked, and he pretty much pulled the same kind of fit he would pull nineteen years later.

It healed. I had a big fancy cast from shoulder to finger that I wore through most of the summer, and then a protective brace made out of space shuttle material to ensure I didn't break it again. I became fascinated with orthopedic surgeons and bones throughout the process, and would base my next county science fair project on the two hundred and six bones that make up our skeletal system. In the research, I also found that when a bone heals, it creates new bone around the break, making the broken bone stronger than it was before and likely stronger than the bones around it. People are like bones in this regard, I think. Breaks likened to heartache. If you can let God heal your broken heart, you can become one of the strong ones. But I digress.

He made me get back on. It was fall. Another Sunday. Pretty leaves. Jeans. Princess was saddled this time. And I was the mule. Squaring off with my father next to the hay swing in our front yard.

It is the gosh-darned pits to be born into a family where you're the only one who's not brave. My mom may look delicate, but she's not afraid of anything. My dad trained for the Olympics in boxing. It never occurred to my sister to be afraid. But I am. I run through scenarios in my head until it hurts and have to force myself to be brave. Probably the reason I think bravery is probably the most attractive quality in a person.

So they were all kind of attempting to force and root me on, knowing how important it was to get back up. My sister was the only one who took any pity on me.

"You don't have to, Sissy," she said. But she's always been the enabling one, so...

"One time," my daddy said, "Just one time. I'll hold her, and I won't let anything happen." I didn't trust him. Not because I thought he wouldn't do everything in his power to protect me, but because as a savvy ten year old, I knew some things were out of my daddy's control.

But I got on. I sat on that girl for about ten minutes while my dad led her around the yard, and I clutched the pommel on the saddle, praying. He helped me off, and I went in the house to read a book.

I wouldn't get back on for another eleven years, at another time to prove that I could, forcing myself to be brave.

Attempting to get pregnant again was like that. Wanting it so bad but being terrified of the possibilities. Forcing myself to be brave. Getting back in the saddle, stone cold sober this time.

Julia Roberts is Not a Drug Addict

joy
/joi/
noun
1. a feeling of great pleasure and happiness

I asked for an epidural. I don't know why. In retrospect, it seemed like the right thing to do at the time, like if I could keep checking things off the list, the sooner we'd be finished.

Like I said, I had been planning on going drug-free. I have a heavy aversion to painkillers. Drugs aren't made for my system. Downers make me high. Uppers bring me down. Every single flipping side effect that comes with a drug usually affects me. I'm that stellar one percent that confounds practicers of modern medicine. Most "painkillers" don't work and in the interim, turn me into a raving lunatic. After my first knee surgery, I would come home every day from high school and cry while I sat in the mechanical mobilizing device designed to make sure my muscles didn't atrophy and my ligaments didn't stiffen.

"Why are you crying?!" my mother asked in dismay.

"I don't know!" I shouted, delirious. "It's got to be my straight A's, or my beautiful hair, or my popularity. Or maybe it's the, count-'em, six boys that keep calling me and sending me flowers because they're in love with not only my Julia Roberts' likeness, but my inner beauty and toughness."

"It's the drugs!" Her eyes gleamed. "I'm calling the doctor."

She was right. They stopped giving me narcotics, subbed over the counter ibuprofen, and the crying jags stopped. They weren't really helping the pain anyway.

I promise I'm not just a wackadoo. My grandfather suffered from the same issue. My grandmother will swear to it. He once tried to, somewhat successfully, attack a male nurse after they'd given him a shot to make him go to sleep. He grabbed him by the collar and almost lifted him off the ground. This, from a man who had no use of his right arm for years. Go figure.

So, with the good sense I had about myself, I had decided to forego pain meds. I could handle it. I've been in a lot of pain before. I could deal. In fact, when I was ten, I used to have stress-induced colon spasms. They told my mother I felt like I was giving birth. I thought, hey, I've done it before, I can do it again.

But this was different. They kept telling me how liberal they would be with pain management and that the epidural would be optimal to keep me calm. I wasn't getting a kid out of this deal, so what was the point of sucking it up and toughing it out? Nothing. So I said, "Let's do it."

It was no big deal. Fo' real. I was really concerned about the needle and was very internally nervous, causing my blood pressure to spike like nobody's business, but it wadn't no thang. It would have been great. Had. It. Worked.

They kept telling me it was controlled by gravity, so I needed to concentrate to make sure I was even, and if I wasn't, to tilt myself toward the leg that wasn't as numb. So I did.

By the time the new (we had gone past twelve hours at this point) nurse came in to give me my third go-round of that pill-into-the-cervix routine (we were now at a double dose), my left leg was leaden and my right leg was wide-awake and twitching. She "tilted me." It didn't work. I begged to be rolled onto my right side (I needed relief on my back, which had been in a prone position for forever). It didn't work. They told me to use the hand pump to give myself more drugs. It succeeded in only making my left leg more numb, and didn't work. They called the anesthesiologist to give me something else. It didn't work.

Eighteen hours in and unbeknownst to me, my dad started having a panic attack. Apparently my mother had almost died at this point in her labor of giving birth to me, and it was wrecking him. He grabbed my mother and marched her down to the desk and made her give the story. They nodded and, so I'm told, looked at her like she was crazy. My dad apparently wasn't paying attention to their reactions, because he then made her give them my medical history of things "not working right" on me, and when she was finished, took it upon himself to tell them they better have a back-up plan.

A very stoic, no nonsense nurse, told them there was no back-up plan, that eventually it would work, and it might take another forty-eight hours, but that was the only plan. They would have to wait.

Beautiful little liar.

Ten minutes later she was in my hospital room under the guise of "checking me" and giving me another double dose of that worthless little pill. I was in labor at this time and could feel everything on my right side, my left scarily numb. She told me I was only dilated to a four. She then did what, apparently, no other nurse had been brave enough to do. She very deliberately and without feeling, broke my bag of water. I said the "F" word and threw up.

It was not my finest moment, but she was so *mean* and uncaring. I wanted to kick her with the leg that worked, and would have, had she not been holding it down. Having your water manually broken is the worst pain ever. Worst. Pain. Ever. Trust me, I've been in all kinds of pain. Worst.

I asked her if they could move my blood pressure cuff to another arm, it was hurting me. No. She looked at me like I was an idiot. Your IV is on the other arm. Won't work. She turned around and left the room. I hated her. Everyone else had been so nice. She sucked.

Later, after it was over, she found both my mom and dad in the hall, and talked to them for well over an hour. The same thing had happened to her. The worst part was that everyone just allowed her to sit and wait. She knew I'd had enough. All those other nurses, nice as they were, weren't brave enough to make me endure terrible pain to speed up the process. She had the guts to do it because she knew it was better in the long run. Sometimes it pays to be mean.

Mourning Joy

"Be very careful to really mourn and openly talk about every aspect of the tragedy; as wounds that aren't transformed will be transferred, usually on those you love due to proximity."

– Grant, Caswell's daddy

Joy is mentioned approximately 153 times in the Old Testament, depending on your version of choice. New Testament, 63. Joy, obviously, is important to God. When I found out my son had died inside my body, I lost it. My joy. What I *thought* was my joy. I think I'd often akinned joy to naiveté. My life had its hardships up until that cold February morning, but nothing I felt was beyond my control. As a type-A personality, I felt I could will things into being, just on the premise of my sheer work. Sure, I hearted Jesus, had heard Him speak, had seen God do Big Things. But nothing until this point would rip right through to the core of me and cause me to question my very existence.

Kalan Chapman Lloyd

Why? This was a not so rhetorical question I would begin to pose to myself driving home from the hospital, ready for the twenty-four hour wait before Cas' induction. Why? What was the point of me being alive? I'd accepted Jesus; I was saved. I didn't understand the point of such heart-wrenching, soul-wringing physical pain. It made no sense to me. Why would God leave a believer to suffer? Why didn't we all just go "poof" once we'd found our Savior. But I just did not get it. And I questioned it over and over again. I was like the unfortunate person who had opened Pandora's box and pulled the curtain back on the wizard. I wrestled and wrestled and flapped in the wind, until I gave up.

I really just gave up on a real relationship with God at that point. I didn't have an answer. There wasn't anything I could find that would soothe my soul. So I decided that having faith for me, in that moment, meant not having that answer. I didn't trust God at this point, but I decided that I'd fake it 'til I made it. It was the only thing I felt I could do, given that I knew from personal experience there was a God and He did Big Things. I decided to rest on that awhile and see where it took me.

But the joy, or what I thought was joy, was gone. I looked at events and experiences with shrouded eyes and a heavy heart, waiting for the other shoe to drop. For myself, for others.

How very, very sad is this? This passive resignation to just believing there's a God. As a teenage Baptist in Oklahoma, this would be a terrible plight. One they would talk about while waiving their W.W.J.D braceleted wrists. Lukewarm Christian, bad. On fire for Jesus, good. Imagine the guilt as a twenty-something, then. Imagine the inadequacy when you discover your giveadarn so broken you can't even muster up any good guilt. And I was living with a former Catholic.

Fire and Rain

Petrichor: The smell outside after it rains

– Webster's Dictionary

I had called my mom on my one-month anniversary, worked up and anxious, and tried to get her to confess.

"Is there something wrong with me?"

"Yes, of course. Lots of things. What in particular are you referring to?"

"Well, I had sex. And I'm not pregnant. Did that Scarlet Fever when I was two make me infertile?" My mother had the very nerve to laugh.

"There is nothing wrong with you. Go have a glass of wine and relax." If only getting pregnant was that easy, y'all. I was on every message board on the web trying to determine if I was ovulating, starting to ovulate, done ovulating, had early pregnancy symptoms (which are mysteriously like PMS). The two-week wait became an agonizing time. For two months.

I try not to feel too guilty about the fact that I get pregnant from a margarita and a raised eyebrow. Three very charming times. If you're ever in Tulsa, go have a margarita at Café Ole's. Or don't, you know, if you're not interested in being knocked up. No one wants our story. Getting babies into this world is hard. Birthing death is the worst.

Even through all the contractions and a crazy, unpredicted thunder and lightning storm, I managed to fall asleep. The nice nurse that was too wimpy to break my water earlier shook me awake.

"He's coming."

"Do I need to do anything?" I asked her, in a stupor, but wanting to be brave, for him, for my son. She shook her head.

"No, you're okay."

So I lay there. With my husband rubbing my forehead until it was raw and my hair was greasy. With my mom holding my hand. And with God making my body blissfully unaware of any pain. Less than an hour before, I was in full-on contraction mode, but God had come down and blanketed my body to take away the physical hurt.

And so, he came in to the world with a bang, like we'd known he would. Caswell Thomas Lloyd; born on Leap Day of 2012 at 5:50 in the morning, just as the sun was bursting through a crazy storm that had threatened to shut off the electricity of the hospital. After twenty-four hours of horrific, unimaginable pain and trauma, his body had been delivered. I had not cried. I had been brave. I had endured. I had survived.

Then they asked me if he had a name...

I burst into tears, trying to be valiant, trying to be honorable to him, to his memory.

"His name *is* Caswell Thomas Lloyd."

Later, Grant would say that the unexpected storm was God crying with us, for us, mourning for us as we mourned for our dead child.

Tears are cathartic, washing away angst and unrest. We wash our hands to cleanse from unwanted germs. The water and the soap taking away the bad. Rain falls, from Heaven, bringing new. I've always liked rain. My great-grandma used to tell me that thunder was just God's tater wagon and lightening was a fireworks show in Heaven. We had a big wraparound porch growing up and on Sunday afternoons, during storms, my daddy would make "hors dee vors" (bologna, cheese and crackers), and we'd sit outside and watch (can you say Redneck?). My mom would always let us play in the rain; puddles were never an issue for her.

I still like rain. God's tears, or the pleasant remembrance of a missing piece. As the farmers say, "rain is a good thing."

A Baby Story

"Is everything okay?"

Coming back from that resounding, world-stopping, earth-shattering "NO," is something I will struggle with for the rest of my life. I barely survived the first time. I know that bad things CAN happen. That can really cloud out the good times, if I let it. The good news is, I'm getting better at it. It's still a matter of life and death. I still brace myself for the unimaginable. I still desperately need to hear the words. Now I'm just a little braver and more upright when I stand up and take it.

– Sam, Lily's mama

Hindsight is always ever so clear. Looking back, I knew something was wrong with the kid. He'd been wiggling away for quite some time, and then had stopped. His normal 3pm workouts hadn't happened for about two weeks. Even a real Coke didn't jolt him enough to jab me. I'd consulted people, nonchalantly saying in passing, "He's not moving like he was." Everyone told me that was normal. Grant had asked at his office, and the newer moms had reassured him. The consensus was that he had wriggled himself around and was working out backward and I just couldn't feel it. Besides, I wasn't at the point where I should really feel him anyway.

But I knew something was off. The Friday before our appointment, I debated between calling the doctor's office or not. I had called the Friday before complaining that sugar was making me nauseous, worried I was developing gestational diabetes. They told me to stop eating sweets. Um, duh.

So I didn't call the doctor's office, deciding to "google" to reassure myself. Pregnant women should disable their "googling" abilities on their computers. It only creates unfounded, unnecessary stress and possibilities. I knew this. I knew how bad those mommy chat rooms could confound one's senses and send a lady into a tailspin. But I did it anyway. Most of the hits told me everything was totally fine. I found one hit that had a string about stillbirth and lack of movement being a sign. I still didn't call the doctor. In a very rational, practical and logical moment, I told myself that if this were the case, then our son was already dead and waiting to find out two more days would make no difference. Isn't a mother's intuition uncanny?

So I didn't call. I didn't go to Labor and Delivery. I went to eat fried chicken instead. There's this place in Oklahoma that's famous for its fried chicken. They only take cash. They only serve three sides and the chicken. And you can't drink the water if you're pregnant. Not sure why. Toxic poisons or something of that ilk. We loaded up a carload of friends and headed toward the iconic road trip destination. Y'all, we may or may not have driven two hours for that dang chicken. I accidentally drank the water before we knew to ask for a bottle. Not much. But enough that before we knew the whole story, our friends would feel immeasurable guilt over no one paying attention. Wondering if that was what had happened. It wasn't. But the chicken wasn't mama's, bless its heart.

I had been sick with a horrific cold for almost three weeks. We chalked this up to a pregnancy cold, and lamented that I couldn't really take anything and nothing helped. The Monday of our appointment, I was finally feeling well enough to pick up working out again, having neglected my fitness to nurse my nose and throat.

Staying home that morning, I was super calm, almost eerily so. I packed my workout bag with two sets of workout clothes, something I never do, but felt compelled to do so that morning. Conveniently, we would be taking this bag for our two-night hospital stay. I cleaned and straightened our weekend mess around the house. I put on two special pieces of jewelry, thinking that I would need them if I needed strength. I watched two episodes of A Baby Story.

I remember driving into the parking garage, thinking, *if something bad happens, we will be okay. Please God, let us be okay.*

Pack Your Bags,

We're Going on a Guilt Trip

"Guilt is perhaps the most painful companion of death."

– Coco Chanel

The day we went to the funeral home to sign the papers so they could burn the remains of our dead baby, I stopped talking.

I don't know that it was an official fugue state; I just didn't have words. No words to comment on anything, no words to express how I was feeling, no words to describe the incredibly psychotic thoughts that were going through my head.

I'm letting them burn my baby. I wish I was the kind of person that could kill myself, but I'm too much of a fighter to just die; I would annoyingly fight back. I'm letting them burn my baby. I want my baby.

Kalan Chapman Lloyd

Why is my baby dead, when all the mean, selfish idiots in the world haven't been spayed and neutered? Why is my perfect husband still talking to me, when I haven't communicated with him in over an hour except for a nonsensical shrug of my shoulders?

I continued to not talk while the very nice funeral home director explained everything to us. Protesting only when he suggested we put something in the paper to announce that our infant son had "passed away." I will forever hate that phrase. We had told it to our four-year-old nephew to explain when his grandfather, whom he'd never had a relationship with, had died. The kid had married it and used it in his almost every day vernacular. At four, his purity was untested, but the casualness with which he said it would irritate me.

Grant convinced me that something in the paper would actually be a good idea, so we would have to tell less people. I nodded acquiescence. He was right, the less I had to deal with well-intentioned idiots, the better.

It was only when the well-intentioned funeral director told us that he'd put a nightlight and a teddy bear with the tiny body of our son that I lost it. I sobbed uncontrollably (this sounds soap opera dramatic, I know, but truly, it was. We were in our own Lifetime movie.). Like he thought that material things such as a nightlight could comfort my kid. My kid was in Heaven; he'd been in Heaven even before we knew he was dead. He didn't need a damn nightlight or a frickin' teddy bear. He offered us a replica of the bear to take with us. We ignored him.

My legs caught while we were walking toward the door.

I was leaving my baby. Leaving my baby, letting them burn my baby.

We got to the car, and I flipped on Grant. "I want that bear." He hesitated and I screamed at him, choking on my words and the tears. "Go get me that bear!" He put me in the car and walked back in to the place where the body of our dead son lay, waiting to be cremated.

His tiny, precious, malformed, non-functioning little heart, hands and feet. His precious feet. His feet were precious. One was perfect and skinny, like his parents. The other was fat and flat, like that of a baby with Down's Syndrome.

Once Grant handed over the small brown teddy bear with the disturbingly intense lifelike stare, I held on to it like a *Titanic* life preserver. Grant tried to take it away, and I mulishly held on. His plea of "he was my baby too" did nothing to deter me from clutching the bear like it was my baby.

Home, I managed to make it to the bedroom, where exhausted and manic, I lay on the bed, mute, guilt settling over me like a comfortable cocoon.

I'd left him. I'd left him at the hospital, and I'd walked away and left him at the funeral home. I'd left him. I was a terrible mother. What kind of mother does that, just leaves her baby? Left him, left him, left him.

When both Grant and my father tried to get me to eat, or pee, or just get out of the bedroom, I refused. Had I had the strength, I'd have punched them both in the face each time they woke me up from a blissfully numb nap to "check on me." I finally told Grant that I'd eat when I got hungry, I'd pee when I needed to, and I'd get up when I could.

And I did. Eventually, I got hungry. Eventually, I had to pee, and eventually, I was able to haul my heavy legs over the side of the bed, push myself up and make my way in to the living room. I didn't eat much, but I ate. I only stayed out of the bedroom for about an hour, but I did. I won't bore you with the quantity of my pee.

The next day was better. I got up, I got dressed. I cleaned out a drawer that had lay untouched since our wedding day while I waited on my husband to take me to my primary care doctor. I made a super intense list of questions to ask my doctor on the day I finally got some answers about our kid. This was based on hyper-aggressive research conducted by me.

I asked my husband to bring me home a yellow legal pad. As an attorney, that yellow legal pad was like the security blankets of all security blankets. Once we'd landed at the diagnostics lab to have an ultrasound to make sure I didn't have a blood clot in my leg (I didn't by the way; it took me another week and a half of excruciating pain in my leg to discover it was my sciatic nerve. Epidurals are a bitch, but you've heard that story.), I had filled up four pages of beautiful yellow paper.

In researching guilt, I came across an epiphany-inducing statement by Dean Jackson. "Never in the history of humankind has guilt changed the thing about which one feels guilty." So very true. My other therapist for the slightly less crazy moments wisely told me that thinking and wondering about milestones in Cas' life was pointless because they were never to be. To play the "what if?" "where would he be?" "what would he look like?" games was illogical. Trying to assign blame to someone or myself was also a losing game.

Lipstick Makes You Taller

"Pretty is as pretty does."

– My mama

I had two things on my mind the day before my first post-partum appointment. Three weeks after birthing my dead kid, I was set on: 1) making sure my nails were perfectly French-manicured and 2) ensuring my outfit conveyed smarts, strength and togetherness, even if it was still a size too small. I wanted all those people at the doctor's office to know that I wasn't this person. This person whose kid dies inside her. This person who has to clutch her husband to keep from hyperventilating in their office. This person who has bad things outside of her control happen.

I wanted them to know that I was that person. That person that had two degrees, the hardest finished in less than the normal amount of time. That person that passed the bar on the first try, in record time. That person that survived multiple surgeries on her leg and defied doctor's predictions that she'd never run again and would probably walk with a limp. That person who'd gone to college and lost the Freshman 50 instead of gaining 15. That person that was normally a size six, and had a designer wardrobe, and a tall, iconically handsome, crazy-smart, kind-to-a-fault husband. A person who had overcome all odds and obstacles and had a quiver of character-building experiences to make her tall and strong. Not this other person I'd become, who counted herself lucky to brush her teeth twice a day, who avoided nice people, who couldn't bring herself to eat whenever she thought of the fact that her son had never been destined to walk, or talk, or laugh with her.

I had chosen my OB not because of a fabulous recommendation or lack of name recognition on the county court website. I had picked her because I liked the convenience of the practice locale and then had stalked the female doctors, discovering on Facebook (oh, the power of the 'book) that her hometown was a hop, skip and jump away from mine, and she'd gone to the same college as my parents. Given this, I figured she'd have the same no-nonsense, cut-the-crap attitude I'd grown up in. I chose her on her hometown alone. Because I am that smart.

Luckily, she was a phenomenal doctor, whose recommendations poured in after I'd already committed to her. And she did speak my language, not my poor husband's, with all his questions and fancy words. I stopped letting him come after the first trimester of Vara's pregnancy. I almost let him go to a hearing the day she was born. Bless his heart. But she and I got along just fine, which was what mattered.

"We wait," she said, "we wait on the autopsy results, and then depending on those, probably you all will have to be tested. A lot."

She thought it was genetics. DNA. Likely Down's syndrome. She had thought his ears were "low-set" when he was born and that one of his feet was turned in, both signs of such.

So we waited. We waited to find out what had gone wrong. We waited to find out if it was because of us or just because. We waited. On pins and needles. With bated breath. We waited.

Say His Name

"Yesterday I was clever, so I wanted to change the world. Today I am wise, so I am changing myself."

- Rumi

When one of our very male, cigar-smoking, incessant-coffee-drinking, thrice-divorced partners happened to walk into the kitchen at work while I was getting water, he told me "Sorry to hear about your bad news. That's a tough deal."

Bad news? Bad news! Tough deal? How would you know, you butthead. Bad news is when you find out they didn't total your car, and you have to fix it and then keep it after an accident. Bad news is when you order a lemon cake for your mother's birthday party and they call to tell you they've run out of lemon and she'll have to eat chocolate. Bad news is when your husband tells you that you won't be taking a trip this year because you spent too much money on clothes. Having to birth your dead baby does not qualify as "bad news." Nor do you qualify for being a determiner of it, you idiot.

I said thanks and walked away.

It's important to me that I mention his name. Casually in conversation. I don't have to be mad at people when they don't that way. I can put it out there first to alleviate any of my possible irritation. I set the rules and chalk the field that way. I think it helps. I don't really care. He's our son, and we can say his name anytime we please. But I've stopped trying to get people to get it and have chosen only to hold fast my ground instead.

I receive so much pity and such obviously irritated discomfort most of the time. But as a mother lacking memories, I have to work hard to make him real. I don't tell people about how much he loved Huey Lewis and the News. Loved, y'all, like disturbingly so. I don't tell people about his very strict 3 p.m. workout regimen. Very strict, serious Olympian. I don't talk about my ideas of him as a soldier in Heaven. So I say his name. "Our first son," I say, "was stillborn." People are funny; they act like they feel guilty for not knowing. People who didn't even know me then. Maybe it's a gut check, feeling guilty for their own children and that they didn't hug them extra tight as they walked out the door. I don't know. I've never not had a dead child. But that's about them. Not about me. And it's important to me that I put him out there. Not just A Bad Thing that Happened. But a person. People can deal. Or not.

You'll Be Back

1 in 160 pregnancies.

Stillbirth occurs in about 1 in 160 pregnancies

– American Pregnancy.org

I am amazed by how many people have experienced this tragedy. Our first nurse at the hospital… her sister delivered a stillbirth, and she herself had gone through two miscarriages. The seemingly mean and uncaring nurse that came in and mercifully and painfully broke my water, the exact same thing had happened to her, right down to the precious low-set ears. The nurse I'd never seen until delivery who cried with me when I told them his name and hugged me afterward, miscarriages. The nurse that took over when they moved me to the post-partum wing that urged me to talk about it so I wouldn't have a nervous breakdown six months later like she had, first-born son was stillborn.

We wondered if this was a chicken-egg situation. Meaning that if you suffered this did it make you predisposed to go into the medical field and particularly become a labor and delivery or women's health issue nurse. I thought it probably was.

Until I went to get my hair done. As an aside, this was a brutal decision for me. My hair looked like crud, but I'd only been going to this hairdresser on a recommendation from a friend since I'd been pregnant. She'd only known me pregnant. Now that I was most definitely not, I was almost embarrassed to have to go face her. I needn't have been.

She didn't say a word, until after her third asking of "how are you today?" and my third reply of "fine." Then she broke and called bullcrap on me, and I confessed. Which led to her confession of her multiple miscarriages in the past few years. These were after a perfectly healthy easy conception, pregnancy and delivery of her own daughter.

So I got to say all the things that I was crazily feeling, and she didn't look at me like those feelings would pass or that I was just having a moment. She agreed with me. Which, let me tell you, there is nothing better you can do for a momma of a dead child but to agree with her. Because we're not crazy when we tell you that we're grateful our child is in Heaven with a perfect body, instead of having physical pain on earth. We mean that. Wholeheartedly. We will feel that way forever, not just in the moment.

I chalked her up to being a God thing. Like a reprieve He'd put in my path so that getting my hair "did" would be a little easier. Special for me.

Two weeks later I went to get a massage to try to alleviate the pain from my irritated sciatic nerve. I was trying my best to try to rationalize in my head how this would go down. I was in a very cranky mood, which turns me into overly honest, and I was afraid if or when she asked me if I could pinpoint when the pain started, I would blurt, "When my baby died."

When she asked when the pain had started, I met her halfway, telling her I'd had an "unplanned epidural." How clever am I, right? She let it go, until I'd flipped over, and she was working on my back and she asked if I minded telling her why.

So I told her. She then told me the same thing had happened to her. The. Same. Thing. Right down to the epidural wearing off on her right side. Right down to her daughter having chromosomal abnormalities. I could not chalk this up to a reprieve. There are so many of us out there that suffer this unspeakable grief.

She then gave me the freakin' golden ticket. After, her doctor had told her that women who have stillborn children due to chromosomal abnormalities were more likely to go on and have really healthy pregnancies. Because children with chromosome issues should technically pass much earlier in miscarriage, it is a sign your body is super fantastic at being pregnant, so when a child has no abnormalities, they should be more than healthy, and you can carry them well.

Holy guacamole. Where was this in my fervent Internet research? Why had my doctor not passed this on to me? Why did they not send you home with that outlined in your grief packet from the hospital? I realized then, that they kinda did.

Every single one of those nurses that had lamented and cried with me, all followed their tears with, you'll have a healthy kid, we will see you again, I have two, three, four live children. My hairdresser had a fantabulously cute four-year-old to prove that she could carry a child. The massage therapist had chosen not to, so she'd never know.

I held on to this nugget of information harder than I had that teddy bear. Lord willing and the creek don't rise, come hell or high water, as God as my witness, I was going to have another baby. This one would be born alive. Watch us.

The Why

"People can plan what they want to do,

but it is the Lord who guides their steps."

– Proverbs 16:9

Exhaustingly, I finally got it. Selfishly, I wanted to go back to being ignorant. There is this not so phenomenal thing that occurs when a child is lost. One mother tries to find one mother, any mother, who understands. I found that mother, bless her heart. #meanit. You basically then proceed to suck the life out of them. #sloom. Luckily for me, she was kind enough to entertain all my questions prying into the deepest, darkest recesses of her heart, her marriage and her other pregnancies. #iamaterriblefriend.

I write about my guilt, y'all, but this is how it should be. There is no better bond than motherhood. There is no deeper bond than mothers whose children are in Heaven. A week or two after

Kalan Chapman Lloyd

EVERYTHING CHANGED, we were at an adoption awareness get-together (you can create your own hashtag here, bless my heart), and a woman (whose children were all alive) told me this would become my testimony and God was using this to show his love and my husband and I just got handed a ministry. I smiled wryly and flexed my hand so I wouldn't curl it into a manicured fist to punch her with.

I once heard a well-known speaker discuss the story of Ruth. About how only Ruth's suffering took her to the "good place" which is humility and dependence on him. The gist was, how the heck can you show Jesus to people if all you've ever known is happiness? Um, ouch. Sadly, if I'd heard this before I'd birthed my darling Caswell, I would have nodded sagely right along with her. That's right. Those painful surgeries have made me so empathetic: I open doors for people all the time on crutches. I mean, I really have no patience for people that don't help themselves feel better, but I'll open the door for them. Literal doors, folks, not spiritual ones.

The speaker is so very right. The only thing to do is to take heartache and turn it into ministry. I have been able to connect with so many friends and acquaintances for which the path to motherhood is, was, and will be, so very hard. And once on it, living with your living children makes the road so steep and rocky. Women who wouldn't have wanted to talk to me otherwise. It divides us mothers, unfortunately. If you haven't lived it, you don't get it. If we've lived it, we don't want to bother you with our angst, and we know you can't relate. If you haven't lived it, you don't want to pry, make us cry, and you can't relate.

No advice or admonitions here, but mamas, let's try. My love knows no bounds for the mothers and non-mothers alike that held me in my ugliness without any reference point to the pain I was feeling. I wanted anyone to ask, even if I didn't want them to ask.

But that is the point. That is why we don't go "poof" after a creek dunking. The point is one day there will be a mama, a family, a child in Heaven before we're ready. And she won't Believe. And she will find me. And I will let her suck the life out of me. She will pry into the deep dark recesses of my marriage (survived!), my psyche (scary!), my living babies (not in therapy yet!), and my faith. And I will tell her how it wavered. How I was battered and bruised from the waves of grief that rolled over with no particular rhyme or reason. How I pretended to trust God so I wouldn't scare anyone around me. How God loved me anyway. How He brought me through it. How He is the only reason I'm standing today. How, on the other side, joy exists. The all-encompassing, heart-grabbing, gleeful kind.

That is my new job. That is why. It sucks. I'll do it anyway.

Try, Try, Again

"My soul weeps because of grief;

strengthen me according to your word."

- Psalm 119:28

There was nothing wrong with him. No weird chromosomes. No birth defects, no funkiness whatsoever.

The actual diagnosis was blood-clotting disorders, both inherited and autoimmune. Two of them. And then some weird antibodies indicative of another disorder or syndrome I had no symptoms for, but would likely develop. And lupus, yeah, the opportunity for that.

The fault, then, lay with *my* body. Not with the way the dance of Caswell's went beautifully awry. But with my own abnormalities. Essentially, I reckoned, after letting it all sink in, my body had created clots in the placenta, cutting him off from essential nutrients and whatnot. Essentially, he had starved to death because my body couldn't get it right.

I found all this out while my mother in law sat in the hospital fighting the beauracracy of medical professionals, her newly diagnosed cancer looming over us. I walked over from my appointment to make sure the nurses weren't giving her the wrong medication.

"So that's good, then," she said. "You can try again right away. Get after it, make more babies." I wanted to punch her in the face. I wanted my feelings to be inconsequential. After all, a cancer diagnosis compared to some blood clotting disorders isn't a good comparison. But she didn't get it. Nor would others. I can see how they wouldn't connect the dots. Guilt doesn't occur to a lot of us when the situation hasn't presented itself in our lives.

To me, those syndromes, those disorders, those antibodies, meant my body had killed my baby. The "if onlys" began. If only they'd run these blood tests before we tried to get pregnant. I had *told* my regular doctor. She *knew* about my other autoimmune disorders. *My* research had shown they all linked up. Why didn't *she* test me?! If only we'd had earlier ultrasounds. If only I'd given a better medical history to my ob. If only, if only, if only.

We had one hurdle before I could try to get pregnant again. Because this special kind of antibodies had popped up, I had to go visit a referred rheumatologist to see if that landed me with another diagnosis of Sjrogren's syndrome. So on a Friday morning, my husband and I went to one more doctor to hear the fate of our future children.

No syndrome. No lupus. Possibility that it might occur. Anti-inflammatory diet. We could go again.

My mom was waiting anxiously for the call. She was happy, I was scared. Too soon, she told me that one of my long-time friends was pregnant, and afraid to call me and tell me. She told me I needed to call her, if I could. Mothers suck like that sometimes, always pushing you to do the right thing.

I called her. I congratulated her. It got awkward. I got off the phone quickly. I really was happy for her. I didn't begrudge her that baby. I begrudged her that naïve happiness that comes from never knowing bad can happen. Sure, she was nervous, she confessed, because of what had happened to me. But she wasn't terrified like we were. Her joyful hesitancy came from a place of hope. Whatever good vibes I could dredge up and send her way came from a place of regretful, unwanted knowledge. Ignorance, for mothers, is bliss.

Skinny is as Skinny Does

"You've always been crazy. This is just the first chance you've had to express yourself."

- Louise of Thelma and Louise

By May, I was skinny again. I managed to drop twenty pounds of non-baby baby weight in two months. Go me. Husband thought it was weird that I thought it was necessary to get back to starting weight before starting to try to get pregnant again. I just looked at him. The idea of explaining to someone who'd been hot all his life how daunting it would be to lose forty pounds of non-baby, baby weight at the end of another pregnancy was just too exhausting to me. I dieted covertly.

When my best friend had come to visit me in the hospital, I unloaded on her. I burst into tears as soon as she stepped into the room, and I'm not sure I stopped crying after she left. Hormonal much?

Kalan Chapman Lloyd

"I can't do this again."

It wasn't a statement. It was a plea. "Please don't make me do this again." Because best friends are wont to be nonjudgmental, she told me we didn't have to. We, mind you, didn't refer to my husband.

She'd known me fat; she'd known me skinny. She'd known me when I was too insecure to really get dressed up for a date. Dirty hair, don't care. So she got it. And let me say it. And hugged me.

But I was doing it again. Or going to. Or planning to. Or thinking about trying. She knew this. Good friends, real friends, true friends, are like that. They let you lie to them. They let you cry and lament and be ugly. They fight with you. They forgive you.

My best friend is everyone's best friend. It's a good thing I'm in my thirties or I'd be jealous and we'd all be squaring off over the lunch table. But she's everyone's best friend because she's just such a darn good *friend*. She won't judge you, but she will tell you the truth. She'll love you through your bad decisions and hold on to the hope that one day you'll be back.

I'm not this friend. I'm busy and lazy and have good intentions, but I don't follow through. My best friend growing up had a stillbirth. Best y'all. Like might as well have been sisters we lived at each other's houses like that. And I would have arm wrestled for her allegiance. Not two years after Caswell died, I heard through the best of friends that this friend had to bury her daughter. My heart ached that I couldn't get to her. It wasn't that we didn't still love each other and like each other's time. But I wouldn't have been a phone call she would have thought to make. I should have been.

Through no fault of either, I wasn't. I reached out and I pray and I wait, until/if she wants to talk, and cuss, and lie. I'll let her. I've got an excellent example to follow.

There were six of us growing up. Besties. We all had favorite allegiances along the way, but we stuck together. Ride or die, like a really small gang, and all that jazz. The core of us had met early and we adopted/jumped in a few along the way.

I can remember, before we got to high school, some altercation, where the smallest, mouthiest of us threatened to whip someone (please remember I am part redneck and some of my people deem beat-downs a necessary evil). Of course, the person to whom she was promising the beat-down called her bluff.

"Well," she responded, huffily and without any hesitation, "I may not be able to do it, but *she* will." She had flung her hand in the general direction of the tallest, sweetest, least mouthy of us. Who then promptly sighed resignedly, shrugged her shoulders, and nodded.

It has happened to three of us. That's half. Some of us talk about it. Some of us talk behind each other's backs, worrying that someone is okay. Yeah, you guys, I know you talked about me behind my back. I know you were worried because I didn't wash my hair for two weeks.

My point, other than my best friends can whip your best friends' butts, is that it happens. More often than anyone whom it hasn't happened to realizes. It happens. And those children exist. And they need to be acknowledged. Ours, I'm sure, are like a small gang, if gangs are allowed in Heaven. They are tough, mouthy, sweet and beautiful. Watching over their people. Smiling when we let each other lie.

There's a Sale at the

Piggly Wiggly

"Be truly glad. There is wonderful joy ahead."

- 1 Peter 1:6

Pregnant again. Yep. Knocked up, in the family way, expecting. I had tested earlier than I should have on Father's Day, hoping to give my husband a Father's Day present that would make up for the fact that his first-born son wasn't here, and after a negative sign had spent the day trying to pay attention to my own father and keep an eye on the husband. The next day just ironically, cosmically, Godly, happened to be Caswell's due date. That Monday I figured I'd earned a mental health day, so I stayed home and peed on sticks. *Lots* of sticks. After the third "yes," I texted the picture of it to a friend (I didn't want to excite my husband unnecessarily, you know). She confirmed those faint lines were definite lines. I took a deep breath and forced myself to do a little tushy wiggle in lieu of a happy dance. I called the hubs.

"I knew it," he said.

"Yeah," I replied, my forced gaiety deflating.

"Let's have lunch to celebrate."

I got dressed, fixed my hair and started planning. The anxiety started to seep in. This was the beginning of two years of me not being able to pay attention to my husband because I was living in an alternate reality on pins and needles, trying to feel a cramp, a kick, a twinge, a swish, a swirl. Trying to hold a baby in my body, trying to will my body not to produce a clot, trying to figure out more ways to ensure that my body would function like a normal human being (because those exist). Prayers didn't come. They would have been half-hearted anyway. I was just white-knuckling my way through the pregnancy, through my life.

This is also the part where I went out and purchased twenty pregnancy tests. Don't judge too much, I had coupons. I started carrying them in my purse, checking the little lines to make sure they were getting darker. Y'all, I'd already had a wand in my yoohoo and a heartbeat. I also knew that once my hormone levels leveled, the tests would stop working. That did not stop me from peeing on a stick (POAS if you've ever been a part of the "trying to conceive" community. Hashtag: TTC) at the airport in my fancy suit and heels. It didn't slow me down from whipping it out of my purse at a really gross convenience store. I may or may not have used one at a friend's wedding reception.

Bat Crap Crazy

"Your crazy's showing. Tuck that crap in."

– A friend

I have a friend who's a psychiatrist. Everyone should have one of these. Only if they're nice and non-judgmental. Mine's nice and non-judgmental. We inherited each other because our husbands were friends. I love her like I love cake. At aforementioned wedding reception, she noticed I wasn't drinking champs or eating shrimp puffs and questioned me. I told her I was, but not far along, and we weren't sharing. Because she's nice she asked how I was feeling.

"I feel like crap, which is probably a good thing. But really, I think I'm a little crazy." I laughed and rolled my eyes. This is what I do, people. I say dramatic things and laugh and people who don't know me well don't really understand I'm not kidding.

Because said friend is a non-judgmental psychiatrist, (why would anyone tell their psychiatrist friend that they feel crazy? Why?) she asked why.

"Well, I've been carrying around pregnancy tests in my purse, you know, just to make myself feel better."

"Hmmmm," she said. 'Hmmmm' is not good when talking to a trained mental health professional. Trust me. And then she told me I needed to go see someone. A very specific someone. She got me a referral to one of her mentors, who declared me officially crazy so my insurance would pay for it and started the process of attempting to debunk all the years of crap that led me to the point of POAS in a bathroom outside a gas station.

I didn't want to tell anyone I was pregnant, because I knew that some, less sensitive, okay, *stupid*, people might think that this quickly conceived pregnancy made it all better. That this baby made Caswell being dead go away. Those lines and that word (I tested with all the brands) might be a strong comfort if we'd had trouble getting pregnant, or if I'd had any early miscarriages. But the knowledge that this kid would more than likely be okay because I was immediately put on a regimen of pills for my disorders, diseases and syndromes and termed officially "high risk," only served to further enhance the fact that Cas was perfectly healthy and normal and my body was freakin' allergic to him and cut off his air and food supply.

Womb is the safest place, my butt.

Risky Business

"The secret to being happy is to just wake up every morning and decide to be happy."

– Ruby Lee Sammons

The remedy and solution to the plight of the disordered was baby aspirin, enough folic acid to take down a horse, and an oversharing maternal medicine specialist. When you're high risk, it is work, peeps. Exhaustive, diligent, appointment-keeping work. The upside is getting to see your nugget way more often than regular mamas. I could wallpaper a bathroom with my kids' ultrasound shots.

It seemed too easy. Take this every day and it will keep your baby from dying inside you. I had seen on a very reliable google source [insert sarcasm here] where others were given fancy anti-blood clotting shots in the stomach. War stories, pictures of bruised and battered tummies, miserable mommies. I wanted to give myself shots. I wanted to feel that physical pain so I could convince myself that it was working and that no clots were forming.

But I couldn't. So I kept going to the doctor. I kept taking the baby aspirin like an old man. I kept hyperventilating every time I walked into the doctor's office. I didn't know if it would be worth it.

It was.

Husband had drug me to the counselor at our church the week after Caswell had arrived. I don't remember much of it. I was in crazy-grief mode, and other than a very poignant piece of advice, I have either blocked most of it out or wasn't checked in to begin with. She very truthfully advised not to travel down any path of what "could have been." Because it was "never to be." She said it much better than I remember, but I have clung to it.

When I said I wanted to die with a giggle, she had laughed with me. I was relieved I wouldn't have to go back to see her. I was embarrassed. She'd seen me real ugly, and I wasn't interested in revisiting that. I would send her a Christmas card the year Cowboy was born to prove to her I had my crap together. I would also go back to her to admit otherwise once Sassy Girl was here.

The new one didn't think I was funny. She'd look at me while I babbled. She saw real crazy people. As opposed to fake ones. Her office waiting room was like something out of a movie. At the end of the first of thirty sessions, she decided my posttraumatic anxiety syndrome (or whatever she called it to make the insurance go through) wasn't solely about Caswell. It was about me. My medical history. My reality. My fears. A history, reality, and fears I was currently letting affect my future relationship with the little turkey punching me in the bladder.

I needed to start to deal with things head on, she decided. Since every time something bad could happen, something bad had happened, medically speaking, I was expecting bad. Whoa, something bad. Do you see how I did that there? Attempt funny after I've said something deep so I wouldn't have to deal with it and you wouldn't think I was crazy. I'm good, y'all, you have to watch me.

She asked me why I felt like I couldn't call the doctor whenever I was worried. Because that is what incompetent, silly mothers do. Go running at every little sign or symptom. She told me that was stupid.

Twenty-six weeks was the mile-marker with Cowboy. If we could make it to twenty-six weeks without finding a heart block caused by my wayward antibodies, he was in the clear. I'd had an ultrasound every three weeks since week five. Week five, folks. Before they usually even let you come to the doctor's office to pee on their expensive sticks. The beauty of the high-risk pregnancy. I was so over it. I was tired of holding my breath every time the show started, my chest tightening until I heard the glorious sound of his very fast heartbeat. Other mothers pay big bucks for special 4D ultrasounds. I just wanted the luxury of not having to choose that.

My first ultrasound with the specialist at thirteen weeks (please notice how I talk in weekspeak, people. This is a pregnant thing that turns into months until your children are four.) revealed that the ultrasound tech who had discovered Caswell dead had moved to the high-risk practice. Would you believe that as soon as my sweet, sweet son flashed on the screen, she said the exact same thing she'd said when my baby was dead.

"Awww, he's curled into a ball today."

I don't even have words. Upon reflection, what a dumb thing to say anyway. Who wants to hear their baby is curled into a ball? I thought my husband was going to hyperventilate. Luckily the sound was turned way up high so Cowboy's steady 156 bpms were loud and proud.

I wanted to whap her upside the head. We very quietly ignored her chatter and left the office after scheduling our next appointment.

I'm mean. The photographer who takes all our family pictures has been crazy enough to become friends with me. Whenever we scheduled newborn photos she would send me a detailed to-do list on how to get them to sleep, sweetly and serenely.

I would ignore and do the exact opposite. The second time around she'd done more research and had her own methods. Neither one of my children cooperated with her plan, and I have two very interesting, wide-eyed, very non-newborn, newborn portraits of my children. I never said anything to her, but I silently cheered on their crankiness and awakeness. For some reason, those pictures bother me, the ones with their eyes closed, and they're very still. For obvious reasons. Other people's kids don't bother me in this manner. Swaddle 'em up and shove 'em into a football. Whatev, man. Not mine. I want mine all stretched out and new-baby-weird looking.

"Tell them you don't want her anymore," the head doctor said when I told her about the ultrasound. I was taken aback. Call someone out and make a ripple? That's, like, anti-Southern. It might hurt her feelings. "So? Maybe then she'll come up with some new material." I wrestled with this for about a week until I had to call to reschedule the appointment.

Date redone, I waited until the last second before the scheduler got off the phone.

"Is it possible to request to *not* have someone do the ultrasound?" I asked guiltily.

"Sure!" she said, bubbly, like I'd asked for a lemon with my tea. "Do you have someone you like?"

"Yes! We really like Lacey."

"Lacey's great. I'll make sure you get her from here on out." No sweat. Ask, and ye shall receive the best ultrasound tech of all time.

At twenty-five weeks they found a white spot on his heart. Oversharer that she was, the doctor (who is very kind by the way, it's just my own personality defect and fear that made these visits so annoying) told us, very clinically, that this was a sign for Down's syndrome. There were other markers, of course, that he didn't have, and usually only one indicated nothing, but...

85

Kalan Chapman Lloyd

I wanted to be on a "don't ask, don't tell" policy with the specialist. My regular OB was like that. Our visits were short and sweet and unless there was an issue, she just told me she'd see me soon. Not this high-risk, specially-trained specialist with the fancy special equipment. She told all.

A week later it was gone. Miraculously and mysteriously as it came, it disappeared. No other markers showed up. This happens sometimes, she said.

At thirty weeks, I started going to the high-risk office once a week for stress tests. "Humor," says Mark Twain, "is tragedy plus time." I can look back now at my son in these moments and laugh about how spot on indicative it was to his personality.

He failed. Every. Single. Test. They do two, to check two different things: a baby's reaction to contractions, to make sure their heart rate is responding appropriately. They watch them practice "breathing" in the womb. I would go in and start whatever test they had available first. Cowboy would fail. They would take me into the room for the next test and literally, people, eight weeks in a row, I would be on the verge of having to head my big ole pregnant butt on over to labor and delivery when just in the nick of time, he'd cooperate. I'd started leaving an overnight bag in my car just in case he decided not to mind one day.

On top of this, I'd developed another fancy little tick called "White Coat Syndrome." I'd walk into the doctor's office, sit down to take my blood pressure, and you would have thought the machine had set off bells and whistles the way they'd act. They'd whisk me away to pee in a cup to make sure I didn't have preeclampsia, which I didn't, but the hyper vigilant maternalist was so worked up I finally convinced her that it was just *her*. I went out and bought my own blood pressure cuff, took it home, and it was totally normal. I took great pleasure in calling her office to reassure her I was alive and that she was the one causing it to spike. Don't judge.

One would think, amidst all this drama, the "almost" and the "uh-oh" and the "something wrong" I would have felt like I'd earned the right to call the doctor any time I dang well pleased. I didn't. I'd already laid my crazy card on the table and didn't want anyone to see it again sometime soon. I was playing the hand close. My psychiatrist wanted to explore this. Fan-freaking-tastic.

I Miss Everything About You

"Every once in a while we bring up Hayes Andrew to Parker. We ask her who he is and where he went. It's important to me she doesn't forget that he had already become such a huge part of our lives. Her answers vary from time to time but she never fails to say: Hayes Andrew is our angel baby. He went to Jesus' birthday." Lately she's added, "It's okay Mommy we still have him. He's on your necklace with baby Parker." I had a small angel given to me that I added to a necklace that holds a picture of Parker on it."

– Mandy, Hayes' mama

I wonder sometimes if I make up the memories I have of Caswell. I only have an idea of him. I only have one picture of him. I only have his tiny capsule of ashes. I feel like I know things. I'm his mother. I guess I can make stuff up. Or know that I know.

I know he really likes Huey Lewis and the News. Really likes it. Danced up a storm. He gets that from his grandpa.

I know ranch dressing is his favorite food group. I hope he's eating healthier in Heaven than he was here.

I know he likes to workout and stretch at 3:02 p.m. on the dot. He gets that from his mama.

I know he's handsome like his daddy. His grammy told me.

I know he's watching over his brother and sister. I know he's with us, in our hearts. I know he's protected them from things that have already come their way.

I know he's perfect, as children born straight into Heaven are wont to be.

Caswell's birthday only comes once every four years. Leap Year babies are special in that regard. It's a blessing and a curse for us. We don't have a birthday to get to celebrate. We don't have a birthday to have to mourn. We have ideas about how to mark that four-year roll-around. The day is fraught with possibilities. We haven't decided. So we haven't moved.

Because we are tasked with making memories for him,.. without him,.. the four of us are faced with having to remember or lie. We may lie; that's more entertaining. Poor kid will be rolling his eyes in Heaven.

Live With the Living

"Your greatest contribution to the kingdom of God may not be something you do, but someone you raise."

– Andy Stanley

I want another a baby. Our sweet precious at the writing isn't even five months old. Oh, my heart yearns for another go. Another sweetie to cuddle. I feel like there should be three of them. There are three of them, but I feel like we need three in our house. But I feel like if I had three, I'd feel like I'd need four. And if I had four, I'd want five. There will always be one missing.

We gambled with the sugars we have now. We crossed our toes until week twenty-six waiting to see if a heart block would appear. We pushed aside the possibility of dangerous antibodies attacking our babies in the name of having our own family. Selfish, y'all. I cannot imagine life without them now, so I won't dwell on what terrible parents we are for having risked their lives for our own happiness.

Kalan Chapman Lloyd

So two is it. During Vara's pregnancy, I had every complication under the complicated star system. The doctor told me, not unkindly, that I sucked at this. Pregnancy. I was terrible at it.

So before the chickie was born, I sold most of my maternity clothes on eBay so I could buy a painting for our bedroom. I pushed aside a dream at another baby. Oh, I want one. It burns in my chest. We'd always planned to adopt. We were a home study short of approval to adopt through the foster system when we found out we were pregnant with Caswell. I don't know now. Now, I have to make all my decisions about more children based on the babies I have.

I can't risk another one's life trying to replace the one I lost. I can't disrupt the lives of two amazing people because I feel like *I* want, *I* need. I can't ignore my children here with me, living, breathing, by scrambling around, scattered and scared trying to find them a brother and a sister to adopt. Because it would have to be even, y'all. I couldn't have just one adopted child. The bios would outweigh them. Not fair.

It took me two years to realize, that if there was Cas, there would be no Rafe. There would likely be no Vara. I cannot imagine my life without the sweet balm that is Rafe. I cannot fathom my existence without the sassy thing that exists. Don't get it twisted, man, you can't trade babies. One doesn't replace the other. Every child is unique, and in a perfect world, I'd have all three. But logistically, medically speaking, if I had Caswell in my arms right now, I would never know Rafe. Not okay. The blessings I live with now far outweigh the pain we've endured.

So I live. With what we have. I meet myself where I am. Right now. With them. I try not to wish the days away, yearning for the child who's not here. I try to yearn for the children I have, wishing for more days with them. We teach them about Jesus, we mention Caswell's name, we talk about God's love; so that one day, our family of five will be one.

Two Stupid Questions

"You can't fix stupid."

– Unknown (okay, every Southern mama I know)

There are two questions new(ish) parents get asked often. 1) Is this your first? 2) How many kids do you have?

Um, why? What is the point of this? If you only have one, are they going to feel sorry for you? If you have three, are they going to feel sorry for you? If you have two, are they going to wonder if you're having another? If you have four, are they going to judge you? If it's your first, are they going to offer unsolicited advice because you. Know. Nothing? If it's not do they assume you don't need any advice because you've. Seen. It. All? Yes. And then some.

People, humans, with their many intricate languages, and lofty theories and self-sufficiency, do not know what to say, typically. These questions are innocent and my irritation likely induces eye rolling, but it is so very, very awkward being a family of five in this world, when there are only four of you on the family Christmas card.

It is so awkward being that mother pregnant in a business meeting and the client asks if it's your first. First what, rodeo? I cried in the bathroom by the way, kept my tongue and the client. It is so very, very awkward for anyone that's lost a child. So stop asking.

Start saying. Questions are lazy communication anyway. Say things. "Your kids are adorable." "You are a beeyooteeful preggo lady." "Your husband is so lucky."

People say the darnedest things. It is at the most inadvertent times that a mama can get hurt. I've been the most hurt by what people say about themselves. Our lack of self-reflection and self-involved selves can be so very hurtful. Self-reflection is hard. I know why people don't do it. No one wants to peel back the layers of their own onions to realize they don't have all their crap together. My advice is to just take a knife and whack 'em.

Just Do It

"If you flinch and turn away, it will smack you. And it will hurt like a sonofagun. If you face it, with your eyes on it, you can catch it. And that don't hurt."

– My childhood softball coach, in reference to balls flying at my head

As previously discussed, I have a fear of appearing crazy and anything less than competent. Never mind that whatever strangeness is swirling up there in my head is probably more than evident to those around me. I'd like to think no one can see that crap.

I borrowed a friend's baby heartbeat monitor at thirteen weeks pregnant with Rafe, the first time it's said to work. I checked his heartbeat every day. Every. Darn. Day. I took it on vacation. I took it to work. It became like brushing my teeth. I did it while brushing my teeth.

Kalan Chapman Lloyd

They say there is a healthy *range* for baby heartbeats. That is great in theory. If you're not a mom in a panic about your baby being born alive. Rafe continually hovered at 156 bpm. If the monitor (which was an at least thrice handed down Craigslist purchase) showed 144, I panicked. If 172 flashed, I started the spiral. I'm being real on the numbers, people. I remember being on a shopping trip with my mom and counting his hourly movements, which didn't satisfy me. Probably because it was too early to measure. I hid from my mom in the bathroom the first three times I checked his heart rate. I gave up the hiding so she could help me try to calm down. It's so funny now to think of me being afraid to appear to be vulnerable and crazy in front of my mother. This is the woman that has seen me at my absolute, utter worst. But I didn't want my fragile shell to crack in front of *anyone*.

My therapist told me to get over myself. Since I was living with the self-created guilt over not having called the doctor when I "knew" something was wrong with Cas, in order to change that perspective, I was to take full advantage of the doctor when she told me to call over anything and everything.

So I did. Finally, slowly, with great groaning pangs. Bless her heart. Bless mine. Bless it all. After eating a lukewarm hotdog at a college football game and getting heartburn, I called her before we left the stadium to make sure I didn't have listeria poisoning. Every time I had a cramp, a spot, a sneeze, a cold, I called her. Ironically, pregnant with my daughter, I felt a little more "chill" but ended up hospitalized twice for the stomach flu. She came out with a beautiful head of hair, though. Worth it.

I fixed a salad one day for my nephew and then left him with my husband, heading by myself to the hospital for some mysterious pain. It was like a test. A test to see just how brave I could be. Just how nuts I'd let them think I was. Surely, they talked behind my back, but they were nothing but kind and solicitous while I was there. The pain was a growth spurt. A flippin' growth spurt. Another telltale sign of what was to come. No one laughed. I didn't die of shame and embarrassment.

I discovered that when you went to the maternity and delivery ward, no one thought you were crazy. In fact, some of my curtain mates had much more interesting stories than I did. I also discovered their emergency room is much, much better than the regular one. I discovered that competency did not lie in pretending to know everything was okay, but going to find out if everything was okay. This is the way of any lawyer worth their billable salt. Don't know everything, tell them you'll find the answer. I take this approach with my babies, self and husband now. Those poor kids are on a very personal basis with their pediatrician's practice. Only once have they told me it's just a cold and to go home and cuddle.

I now believe in being a proactive mama. If nothing else, I get to find out how much my future football player weighs that week.

Forgiving

the Well-Intentioned Ding-Dongs

"To err is human; to forgive, divine."

– Alexander Pope

There were three people I wanted to punch in the face after my son died. One involved accidental mail. One involved intentional, ill-worded mail. And one I won't give details because I love her still, and it would kill her to know she hurt me.

I held on to this crap and clung to my righteous indignation through the pregnancy and birth of my second son. It burned, and when it wavered and threatened to blow itself out, I re-ignited it. I needed someone to be mad at. And these people, these terrible, awful, insensitive, unkind people needed beat-downs (redneck term). They needed to suffer. They should hurt like the hurt they caused.

I was holding buckets of water with no break. My arms got tired. These "people," while I stood in the flames burning, never knew they'd hurt me. Never. Knew. It. They weren't suffering. I was.

So I decided to forgive them. And then discovered I didn't have the capacity. Because we don't. We don't have the ability to forgive the morons, the mean people, and the sinners. Only God has that quality that steps in and forgives *for you*. We don't forgive. We're the forgiven.

He forgave me for the terrible thoughts I had after my child died. He forgave me for the railings I'd subjected my husband to. He forgave me my doubt. He forgave *for* me. He forgave *me*.

Running, and Running, and Running Away

"Blessed are those who mourn,

for they will be comforted."

- Jesus

Psychologists have the grieving process boiled down to a fairly simple checklist. If you can move down through the items, you can get on with your life. Easy enough, right? But this is where most people get "tuck," as my toddler would say. I have a friend that fully embraced grieving. She cried, she wailed, she posted on Facebook. She got right down in the muck and mire. She was judged rather harshly. "Dramatic" was the word de jour. But several years later, she's one of the healthiest mamas I know.

Still another, is "tuck." Grief isn't a thing you can time, it isn't something you can plan; yours isn't something that looks like anyone else's. But this other friend seems angry and frantic. She appeared to be searching for ways to fill the void, to find answers, to do something to make a difference, wound so tight that at any second she might snap.

She was just mad.

I think; when you let God fight your battle, when you let him hold you while you weep, when you finally get your faith back to believe in life again, the anger goes away. By the way, this applies globally to anger, not just the grieving kind.

There is absolutely no way anyone can ever find peace the death of a child without the knowledge that your little one is tucked safely away in Heaven with your people (your people is southern for "family and friends-like-family"). Our Father is here to hold and comfort us and take away the angst. If we run away from that, we're running away from the soul-deep safety that only God can hand us.

Running away isn't special to people who don't believe. There are those of us with what people would assume have a good solid Christ relationship that get dazed and confused and start directing our anger at the most worthless of places. But like the Prodigal Son, spending all your money, honey; if we get down to the very end of ourselves and let God call us home, there is comfort in His arms. But I think you have to go through it. It has to be gut-wrenching, soul-searching, messy and gross, before it can be glorious.

You Dirty Little Hope-Haven, You

Hope is the thing with feathers that perches in the soul and sings the tunes without the words and never stops at all.

- Emily Dickinson

There it was again. That little niggle. A flutter of happiness. I kept trying to handily slap it back down. After tragedy strikes, we clutch and grip at "maybe" with bloody fingernails and sweaty palms, all the while cocooning ourselves in protective pessimism. One foot in the ground, one toe on the grass; a game of physical and mental Twister. When God pushes us to toward hope, we shrink back into the shadows; reality and remembrance the garlic of pregnant women.

We decided to name him after the archangel Raphael. We needed a bad-A kind of hero namesake to convince ourselves this kid would come out kicking butt, disorders be damned. A cousin took Gabriel the year before and Michael was a family name with unpleasant memories. In a twist of perfection, Raphael happened to be the patron saint of medical workers. Grant's Catholic family got behind it.

Grant wouldn't agree to the full treatment of the name so we settled on Rafe. With his middle name after his Papa, a nod to all things brave. I refused to go all-in on imagining him. I had put expectations and labels on Caswell, I had set him up for failure. Thank goodness that kid's in Heaven and perfect; he'd have never lived up to the standards we'd created for him in the twenty-four weeks we knew of his existence. I didn't want to do that to Rafe. He was Rafe and his humanity was his to do with as he would.

But I hoped, skeptically, periodically, and guiltily. I hoped. I hoped he was strong. I hoped he was brave. I hoped he knew Jesus loved him. I hoped he was handsome, and then awkward in his teenage years so girls wouldn't turn his head. I hoped he lived. I hoped I wasn't crazy for having hope. Hope is the thing we cling to when we lose our faith. It's that little nudge, that push, that says "maybe," "perhaps," "almost," when reality stands on the other side saying "no" and "never." It's the foundation on which our faith is based. It's where God finds us.

I hear people often talking about "standing in the gap" for someone by praying for them. That's God. He does the things we can't do. He carries us. He holds us. He forgives. He loves.

Birds, Birds, Everywhere Birds

Beside them the birds of the heavens dwell;

they sing among the branches.

– Psalm 104:12

Things are important. If one is living, they are not. Our consumerist society gets the guilts and throws stuff out, only to start anew. At writing, Rafe is a year and a half and I've already made a lot of money selling his old stuff, and he has a baby sister. I've saved a few special shirts from trips his grandparents went on or took him. But for the most part, it gets shucked when it's not usable in our house anymore.

I have a box of Caswell's things. A very fancy box my wedding china came in. Someone I don't remember was generous enough to buy us a whole place setting instead of just a few pieces and the box is nice and big and sturdy. Clean and white and just big enough to hold all of his *things*. I once saw a new mother on a reality show who came home after delivering an early arrival exclaim, when she saw that her family and friends has finished the nursery, "we have things!" It seems vapid, but I get it. That's what you do in pregnancy. You hunt, gather, peck. Because you have so little control of what's going on inside your body the comfort comes from washing and folding tiny little white onesies. From researching the best laundry detergent. From calling your best friend at 6am on a Sunday to ask if you can iron said onesies because they're wrinkled. No, by the way, that means you've washed too many. Always ask another mom.

The purchase of these things would haunt me in our second pregnancy. I would fill an online shopping cart, or a basket at Target, then leave it in the frozen food aisle, or exit out of the page. I would get reminders from The Gap and Carter's, beckoning me to "come back" and not leave my shopping cart behind, discounts and incentives flooded in.

I finally decided it would be some sort of tortuous therapeutic exercise if I gave them my credit card number and had a whole box of baby crap shipped to our doorstep. I didn't know yet that Rafe Alan was a Rafe Alan and that he would look terrible in baby yellow. So I bought a full wardrobe of baby-duck accented, cold-weather pieces.

I thought it honorable to refuse the offers of a baby shower. It was dishonorable, to me, given that I didn't believe in showers after the first baby. We decided to have a sip and see after he arrived. I wanted one, a shower. I wanted the silliness, the attention lavished on my baby and me, the diligent registry-making. But most of all I wanted to be normal. I wanted to not already be the mother of a baby I didn't have.

Caswell's things don't fill up the box. I think maybe one day it will be full. I thought about moving it to a smaller box after my husband gave me a plate and bowl on our anniversary. I didn't. We add to it. Every time we donate in his name, or someone sends us something in remembrance of him, we add to it. He is a person. His things are important. The custom Switzerland map bib from Etsy, the super fancy expensive Christmas pajamas on sale too good not to buy, a chevron burp rag Grant's cousin had made us.

There is a box within the box. From the hospital. When *this* happens they make sure you have things; cards, baby hats, knitted blanket, prayers, the hospital bracelets marking that awful stay. Things.

The boxes are hand-painted by some unknown person. On Caswell's box is a robin red breast. I imagine it's the European kind. They're prettier. That spring there were what seemed like a million baby robins swarming our yard. Little baby birds struggling to grow, to learn, to become. I would come home and find one waiting on me as I pulled into the drive. My baby saying hello.

Those baby robins in the spring were fat and sassy by fall. Strong, plump and clever. Comfort came in the form of watching them scratch and swoop and eat hearty. My worries of Cas growing and learning and being were erased. When I see a robust robin, hanging around me, as they do so often, I am reminded that my son grows, he learns, he is.

Birds are now the bane of my existence. When my husband's mother was on the verge of passing away from cancer, a blue jay kept trailing my husband, pecking along near him whenever he was outside. My grandfather died the day my daughter was born. The Saturday before, we had Rafe and a nephew at a park and a weird-looking white and brown speckled bird came hopping up to me. I knew then it was coming. No, my grandpa wasn't anything but handsome, but I just knew. I've yet to be able to identify that bird, which is telling.

When a robin hangs out by the tree in front of our house, it's a sweet reminder that Cas has come to visit. When I see a bird new to our yard, I start to get a little freaked out, worrying about who the bird might resemble. There's an Alfred Hitchcock movie I always think of, which has nothing to do with my circumstance, but I can put myself in a spiral faster than you can say "boo" about birds coming to swarm my house.

But keep the robins coming. Their song is so, so sweet.

My Dad Won't Stop Crying; and Other Necessary Annoyances

"You can cry about it... Or you can dance about It."

– Kid President

My dad has acute crybabyitis. Meaning he cries all. The. Time. Happy tears, sad tears, angry tears, you name it. He has turned into a softie in his old age. The man is 6'4" with a barrel chest, saddle leather skin and calluses that would cut you like a box blade. It would be comical if it wasn't so awkward and didn't happen All. The. Time.

My mother pats him and rolls her eyes. When I was in the hospital to produce Sassy Girl, there was some confusion about who would be coming to the hospital first, given that the boy had developed an infectious virus just in time to not be able to go to school on the day his sister was to burst forth. I was waiting on my mom before I asked for the epidural, afraid I'd have a baby lickety split without her there. They sent my freakin' dad, who was already in tears, having made the rounds with his best friends, the nurses.

I swear to all that is Holy, I wanted to punch him in the face. I think I told him to take his tears and haul his happy butt back to my other baby. He's not the one you want holding your hand when you need to be tough. That's my mom. She's the lady that tells you to suck it up, buttercup and then holds you when it's over.

In the distant recesses of my mind, in the corners that I've shoved the shadows into, I remember them, helpless and hovering, when we went to deliver Caswell. My pain, so very consuming, didn't allow me to see theirs. I could only think of me and my poor plight.

The people that love me the most got shoved away in irritation and anger as I wallowed in the terrible muck that is grief. It's okay. It was what it was. In retrospect, I guess I could have let them love me more. But I couldn't.

We strike out at those that are safest. If someone is lashing out at you, directing their misdirected pain your way, consider yourself ohsoveryloved. No small comfort, but it's the darn truth. You're not going to be mean to people you have tenuous relationships with. The stronger the bond, the bigger the bite.

But could we please cease with the constant waterworks. I mean, seriously.

Good Things Come

To Moms Who Wait

"Our willingness to wait reveals the value we place on the object we're waiting for."

– Charles Stanley (Isaiah 64:4)

I couldn't find my mom. In this story. She seemed to be "in the wind," missing. Odd, because she's a vivid character, central to *my* story. Until I figured out, throughout this part of my story, and so many other parts, she was *waiting*.

Waiting on me. Standing on the sidelines. Praying me on. I have no shocking exchanges or funny anecdotes because there are none. She just believed in me. And prayed for me. And waited for me.

As a mother with a child in Heaven, we think we're special. We are. But. We aren't. As mothers, at some point, we will likely all be separated from our children. Geographically, physically, emotionally, mentally, spiritually. It is a terribly difficult thing to be separated from your child, regardless of where they are, or how far away they are, or why they are far. The mama adopting here, there, everywhere; waiting to meet her baby, waiting to take her baby home. The mama with the prodigal daughter, praying for that baby, waiting for that baby to come home. The mama with the child in surgery, waiting to hear from the outcome, waiting to take her baby home from the hospital. The mama with the military son, praying for that baby, waiting for that baby to get home. The mama with the child in Heaven, praying for that baby, waiting to meet that baby, waiting to get home. The mama with a baby who lost a baby, praying for her grief, waiting for her healing.

Seasoned moms will breathe deep, dig in, hold on, and wait. Sometimes a mother's hardest job is to let your baby go. My mama stood on the sidelines; fists clenched and teeth gritted, a smile pasted on her face, silently chanting, "You got this" (Sports Mom). She watched from the porch as I crashed my bike, over and over again, cringing at each fall, but never rushing out to save me. She sat beside the pool, ever watchful, eyes only on me, with a life preserver handy but cleverly out of sight, as I thrashed and sputtered, learning how to swim.

Angry tears, sad tears, and joyful tears; my mom believed in me and knew I could even when I didn't think I could. No matter where your babies are, you still have a job to do. You know who prayed for me when I couldn't? My mom. You know who praised Jesus when I couldn't? My mom. You know who kissed my sweet baby into Heaven when her baby couldn't? My mom.

Wait, mom, just wait.

The Bitterest Sweet

"Mama always said life is like a box of chocolates.
You never know what you're going to get."

– Forrest Gump

I cried for two minutes when they told me our daughter wasn't a boy. I allowed that irrational indulgence for that long. And then after the appointment, went out, with sweaty palms and pits, and a beating heart, and bought twelve bows. And a bow holder. Who knew they had a bow holder? My best friend. Who promptly told me I'd bought the wrong kind of bow holder.

I guess if Sassy Girl reads this one day and is upset, I'll go buy her a tiara. She can be bought, although she is wont to stamp her nine-month-old feet and wave her hands when her Papa doesn't pay attention to her or she doesn't get her way. And she decides to not be chronically constipated on the days she doesn't like her outfit.

My mama says that life is bitter and life is sweet, and the best way to live it is to acknowledge the bitter, but focus on the sweet. The bitter is Rafe not having that special brotherly bond with Caswell (I know about this special, brotherly bond because I'm a brother. Insert sarcasm, but indulge my irrationality.) or Vara not having two big ole big brothers. The sweet is the relationship unfolding between sister and brother, which is like watching a baby bird hatch; it's so miraculous. They. Love. Each. Other. Love. The sweet is those two having a permanent guardian angel, which is another miracle, and a blessing.

One day they'll probably look at me like I'm crazy and say, "You thought we were missing out on something? What is *wrong* with you, mom?"

It Ain't Pretty

When A Heart Breaks

"I think I can. I think I can. I think I can."

– The Little Engine That Could (and did)

Our children know no fear. We work to make sure it's never introduced. Hence, when the larger child gets out of his car seat and his feet hit the ground, he is off, scoffing strongly at the rule of hand-holding. In the church parking lot a few weeks ago, my husband didn't grab him and off he took. I almost killed my husband. Murder. Straight up. In the church parking lot.

The icy hand of gripping, squeezing fear overwhelmed me and my entire being flooded with cortisol, and I was ready to do serious damage. It's easy for me to acknowledge my demons and intentionally face them in ways that I can control. It's a different ballgame when your demons rush up to slap you in the face and dance in glee when you're unprepared. You start panicking and threatening things like death. And divorce.

The pain eases. The vice-like grip around your life and your heart gently goes away. The fear does not so easily subside.

So you start over. You pull yourself out of that abyss and that *place*, because, again, it's not your children's fault their brother isn't here. You go out and buy a bungie cord to attach your child to you. And then you take a deep breath and put it in the donate pile.

You acknowledge the fear again, and pray for God to smack those demons into submission... because dead husbands are messy.

Husbands and Wives

"It's been said, that marriage, is the best of therapy."

- Paraphrased. Dr. Paul Fitzgerald

I have hesitated to delve too much into my husband and his psyche during this time in our lives. His, is not my story to tell. It seems unfair to include him into the wranglings over my soul. He didn't lose his faith. He maintained, believed, and held fast throughout that we would be "okay," that "God had this," and other meaningless-at-the-time clichés.

No, Grant didn't lose his faith. He lost his wife. He lost the take-charge, patient, empathetic, listening, loving person he'd married. He traded her in for a distracted, distant, empty shell that barely more than used him as a vessel by which to get a baby.

His pain, because he is a father, and like a lot of other fathers, gets overlooked. So I didn't want to overshadow it with the darkness of my own path. So I didn't tell his story. The story of The Day his Wife went Cray-Cray. The story of how she blew around, untethered and unhinged by pain. The story of how he had to sit, heartbreakingly so, and do nothing because there was nothing he could do. The story of how she took it out on him… because we take our hurt out on those we love the most.

So I didn't tell it. Because it is *his* to tell. He lived it too, and then had to relive it in tearful evenings after aforementioned cray-cray woman had spent the afternoon writing. So I'll let him tell the story of how he stood steady and firm, ever loving, ever patient, ever kind, while he waited for his children to show up and his wife to find herself.

Maybe he'll hire me as his ghostwriter.

Poop

(Otherwise known as Morning's Joy)

"...weeping may last through the night,

but JOY comes in the morning."

- Psalms 30:5

I was hooked up to a hospital grade breast pump, trying to get my body to acquiesce to doing what the early born boy wasn't interested in making it do. The husband had gone to get me a sandwich (ugh to hospital food), my dad had gone to talk to all of his new friends. My mom was holding her husband's namesake, getting to know him, finally, in a moment of sweet respite. No nurses, no doctors, no lactation specialists, no social workers, no photographers.

He sniffed a little and smiled sweetly in his slumber, slowly opening up his eyes to blink at his Grammy. She sniffed and wrinkled her pert nose.

"That bottle did something," she said. An hour ago my husband had a slight meltdown and had told me to get over myself and my plans. He'd gone to the nursery to demand a bottle and had popped it in the kid's mouth while I tried to figure out how to attach myself to the fake latching system. Rafe had devoured it happily and hungrily. I would give up the ghost a few days later after he solely and firmly declared himself a bottle baby. But in that moment I was clinging to what the well-meaning morons had told me was "best."

My mom, ever in charge and fully competent, pulled everything out to change him. On the hospital bed, for whatever reason. She opened up his stinkiness and discovered the sticky black tar of that glorious first poop. And it kept coming. She held him up by his ankles so it wouldn't run down his back. And he peed, his uncontrollable little man parts spraying the bed, the window, and his Grammy.

"I'm here mama. In all my solid, humanly, messy self. I'm here. Watch me go."

And so it began. This adventure in parenting this sturdy, squirmy b.o.y. Every day, I gird my loins, preparing myself not only for the day's zaniness but intentionally making myself let him go. I think, as a mother who has experienced the pain of losing a child, it is the natural instinct to clutch your living children to you. To hold them and keep them and protect them from the dangers seen and imagined. I work hard not to do that to Rafe and Vara. Their brother's death is not their burden to bear, and my insecurities are not to be foisted upon them.

So every day I pray that God gives me the strength to let them go, to watch them figure it out from afar, to not hover with the proverbial pillow near a tushy, waiting to cushion the blow of the inevitable fall. Success has been achieved for the most part, that the boy is the most independent little cowboy to grace our presence. He'll load up in a moment's notice to go with Papa to shop for cows, he and his dad will walk out the door for "man-dates" without a backward glance, and his allegiance will always fall with he who holds the ice cream. As I write this, at eighteen months old, the kid drives a tractor. A tractor, kids. I love it. And I very well could have crushed it with my fears and almost stifling anxiety had God not stepped in and done for me what I could not do for myself.

I do take great pleasure in changing that kid's butt, though. (It's okay if you're a mom with children in Heaven, who don't. But I'm obsessed with poop, so...). As an early, lusty, hearty eater, that boy has pooped like a full-grown man since 4 months old. I'll take it. Every time I open up a mess, it reminds me that God brings us Joy. In the morning. Through the mourning. *He* brings us through it. We don't find it ourselves; we can't see it ourselves. He steps in and holds us and may drag us kicking and screaming into the bliss that comes after immeasurable pain. Stinky, dirty, gross, glorious, oversized poop is my everlasting Joy.

Before The Airport

"Some glad morning when this life is over, I'll fly away... I'll fly away, oh glory, I'll fly away (in the morning)."

The pain hits at odd places, in awkward spaces. Looking in the rear-view mirror and catching a glimpse of the sweet, shiny roundness of the tanned cheeks of your son, alive. Finding out a dear friend had to deliver her dear son, still. During Christmas, and Easter, and President's Day. On Tuesdays. At noon. Or three fifty-two in the morning. It can come without warning and with no grace. It can create a panicked, sweaty ugly cry while trying to hold it together in the front seat. It can feel like the widest chasm, reaching down into your soul to just...hurt.

When I was pregnant with Caswell, I was also heavily involved in raising awareness for adoption. Sometimes, when I needed a break from the tax code, I would shut my office door and watch "airport videos." Families of those adopting, typically internationally, would wait in eager anticipation for those parents to bring their children home to the loving arms of those who had prayed and waited. Sometimes, depending on the situation, one parent may have gone alone to retrieve the child while the other had to wait with fervent hand-wringing at baggage claim.

Often, there is a photographer in the bunch of family and well-wishers. Sometimes, there is a news crew, or at the very least a smartphone with a video function, zoomed in on that moment when that child bursts forth on the scene, ready to be scooped up in the craziness of overwhelming, unconditional love. It is happy, and glad, and full of hope and good news. Special moments, caught forever. Sometimes they get posted on YouTube and voyeurs like me could share in the pure joy, tears streaming down my face while enjoying an afternoon coffee and waiting on an email.

And then they go home. Where it is painful, and sad, and traumatic and awful before everyone adjusts. I don't use a brief description to downplay it, only to introduce it. The adoption community calls it "after the airport."

I feel like I am "before the airport." My child is away from me, safe of course, but away. We live in the weird limbo of being very far away from Caswell, but resting assured he lives and his life is important.

So we get up. Every morning. And look for the joy. We look for the birds that remind us of Cas. We sigh deep at the infectious giggles from Rafe and Vara, wondering if their brother giggles with them. I think he does. We pray that the story of the little church-builder does build some churches here, although in a different way his mama had planned, of course. We hope for that airport scene like the one in Love Actually, one day. We are before the airport. At times at peace, some days overcome with lip-chewing anxiety. Always missing him. Always wanting him.

But one glad morning… glory, glory hallelujah.

Acknowledgments

My God, oh how you saved me. Saved me from a life of ignorant bliss, and tossed me into the churning angst of knowing what real pain is and recognizing it in other people. Thanks a lot. It's awesome. Not. Just kidding. But really. Thank you for loving me when I was unlovable, forgiving me when I was unforgivable and holding steady while I ignored you and turned my back on you. I am yours, forever.

My husband, bless your heart. We've made it! How life has changed in our short marriage. Let's be boring for the next fifty years. Thank you for never leaving. Thank you for watching football and trying to give me the play by play while I was on the couch and writing, crying, trying to have a moment. #seriously. You are the best thing studying abroad ever gave me. Thank you for loving all our babies. Forever my number two.

My darling Caswell, my sweet, sweet Rafe and my sassy V. You all are the reason for this book. You all have your very own special story that God has written. I cannot wait to see each of yours in God's timing. Thanks for letting me stumble and fall and be a stinky mom one day and a great one the next. I love you to the tips of my toes and the marrow of my bones. #lifeisgood

My parents, thank you for checking your pain while mine raged. Thank you for loving me and always intentionally putting obstacles in front of me so I would know what it felt like to fail. Best. Parents. Ever. Thank you for seeing who I really was, even when I couldn't. We've come a long way, baby.

Kay Lynn and Stacey. Y'all are the best friends a girl could have. You all showed up and cried with me, made me cry, asked all the right questions, all the wrong ones and never doubted I'd get to the other side. I will always owe you. You'll never get repaid. I'll try with cookies.

Brit. You always inspire me. I watched you persevere to grieve and heal and remember. I watched you be real, and hope and live. We're bonded. For.Ev.Er.

Heath. Friend, thank you for being kind enough to clinically assess crazy. And being the kind of friend unwilling to ignore it. And for reading the crazy, and pointing out ways the words could be clearer.

Ashley. Thanks for sitting with me in the dark. After the morning had come, and reminding me how far I'd come.

My doctors, primary, obstetrician, and specialists. I don't envy your job. I don't envy you us crazy mamas trying to muster a shred of dignity while we're going crazy. I know we take it out on you. Thanks for never giving up on us. More importantly, thank you for never giving up on our babies.

Rafe and Vara's ladies. I doubt you all could ever fathom what blessings you are. When you lose a child, it is so very difficult not to worry constantly with a catch in your throat and overprotect (smother!) the ones with you. You all took that away from me. I have never worried a minute about the care they were getting or the love (spoiling!) they were receiving. In your own special ways, you all threw this mama a life preserver. We will love you all forever. Rafe promises to send basketball tickets when he's rich and famous. Vara promises to send you copies of all the traffic tickets she gets out of with her smile and her charm. I want to name you and shout your names from the rooftops. Miss Mindy, Miss Jane, Miss Kristi, Miss Shaq, Miss Shameeka, Miss Katrina, Miss Dereka, Miss Erica, Miss Elizabeth, Miss Felicia, Miss Jamie, Miss Tarinue, Miss Latoya, Miss Hannah, Miss Rosie, Miss Carmen, Miss Lauren, Miss Kaylie, Miss Jerisha and anyone else I've missed. You see! It does take a village to keep a mama sane!

Nurses. You all are special. Thank you for your stories, your support, your acknowledgment and validity of our feelings with each of our babies. I will never know how you do it. We are blessed to have had you.

Therapists. Crazy is just a state of mind. No really. Thank you for offering respect and dignity when I couldn't find it within myself.

You crazy people willing to read this book and give me notes and suggestions. What people I have! Thank you for seeing beyond the depressing read to really give me feedback.

Resources

A portion of the sales of this book will be donated to M.E.N.D. (Mommies Enduring NeoNatal Death). They have a host of resources and are a support group available for grieving mothers to meet and talk. They meet live and virtually. You can find them and their resources at www.mend.org.

Still Standing is an online magazine dedicated to bereaved parents and infertility. They have a host of articles, support, and connections for anyone touched by infant loss and infertility. Find them at www.stillstandingmag.com.

Share Pregnancy & Infant Loss Support is a community for anyone who experiences the tragic death of a baby. Serving parents, grandparents, siblings, and others in the family unit, as well as the professionals who care for grieving families, Share is a national organization with over 75 chapters in 29 states. Services include bed-side companions, phone counseling, face-to-face support group meetings, resource packets, private online communities, memorial events, training for caregivers, and so much more. http://nationalshare.org/

Hannah's Hope offers families who have experienced pregnancy loss a place to find comfort, support, and resources to help in the grieving process. They work to validate the lives of lost babies by affirming that they are valuable and meaningful. http://www.hannahshope.us/

About the Author

Kalan Chapman Lloyd is an attorney and author currently residing in Tulsa, Oklahoma. She enjoys big hair, Supreme Court Decisions on Intellectual Property, hats, the sound of construction and the feel of brand new sweatshirts. Kalan grew up in the small town Tahlequah, OK, where she graduated from Tahlequah Senior High School. She attended Oklahoma State University and the University of Tulsa College of Law and has been a member of the Oklahoma Bar since 2008. She and her husband, Grant, enjoy parenting their strong-willed, left-handed children. She is a Junior League dropout.

She loves Jesus, her husband, her children, and words. In that particular order.

Kalan is the author of the acclaimed fiction series, *The MisAdventures of Miss Lilly.*

Connect with Kalan at www.kalanchapmanlloyd.com and on Facebook, Twitter, and Instagram.

Other works

The MisAdventures of Miss Lilly series:

Home Is Where Your Boots Are

These Boots Are Made for Butt-Kickin'